## PRAISE FOR THE
## *BREAKTHROUGH BANKING BLUEPRINT*

"We've been using the Breakthrough Banking Blueprint for over a decade. It has literally taken us from a mediocre bank to a billion-dollar bank earning over a 2.00% ROA and 5% NIM, and it has brought us the safety and ease needed to weather any unexpected storms. The only time it doesn't advance us is when we start chasing a shiny new object and move away from the fundamentals that have made us strong. Even then, the Emmerich Group brings us back to the simplicity of a well-executed system, and they always pop our numbers to the next level. I'm perplexed about why any community bank would go it alone without The Emmerich Group installing this system—especially during challenging times."

– Patti Steele, CEO, First Volunteer Bank

"In the last three years, the 'Blueprint' has helped us have a breakthrough we never dreamed possible. Assets have grown 44%, loan growth is up 64%, net income has doubled, AND we were ranked #2 by SNL for banks under $1 billion. Best of all, we were named the 2019 Extraordinary Bank of the Year, and our clients are all thrilled to see what our bank in our small community has accomplished!"

– Chris Floyd, CEO & President, First National Bank of Syracuse; #2 on 2016 SNL Top 100 under $1 Billion; four-time Banky™ Award winner; awarded 2019 Extraordinary Bank of the Year by the Institute for Extraordinary Banking

"We assumed that high performance was for 'the other guys.' Then we found the Blueprint and we skyrocketed from a bank that was battling for average to a high level of performance we never dreamed possible. It was a miracle. We had two individuals from our team who took the Accredited Banking Professional course and, while 'practicing,' brought in $20 million in deposits—$15 million of which were low-cost deposits. And we are hitting every single metric every single quarter—something we never did before. I can't imagine any bank that wouldn't want to have this Blueprint. All of a sudden, we're having a blast coming to work every day!"

– Charlie Holland, CEO, Farmers State Bank; Banky™ Award winner

"As a leader, you owe it to yourself, your employees, and your shareholders to challenge yourself to reach unexpected success. The Breakthrough Banking Blueprint will open your eyes to a new way of being. Using this Blueprint, we more than doubled our non-interest-bearing deposits in three years while growing loans over 40%."

– Lloyd Harrison, President & CEO, Virginia Partners Bank; CEO of Delmar Bancorp; Chairman of Virginia Association of Community Banks; four-time Banky award winner.

"For seven years prior to working with The Emmerich Group, our loan growth averaged just over 2%. Since we started applying the Profit-Rich Sales™ Blueprint, annual loan growth has been over 8%. But the best part is, we have developed level 4 USPs that allow us to receive premium pricing while maintaining excellent credit quality. Our yield on loans is between .35% and 1.4% higher than our local peer group. We've made our franchise not only far more profitable but feel that we have a predictable success machine that will keep us safe during good times and bad."

– Keith Knudsen, President/CEO, Security Bank, Laurel NE; Past Chair of Graduate School of Banking, Colorado; named 2017 Extraordinary Bank of the Year by the Institute for Extraordinary Banking

"Most community banks claim that their focus on customer relationships is what gives them a competitive advantage. Unfortunately, while saying that, many of them fail to resist the trap of continuously competing on price while watching their net interest margin eviscerate until there is nothing left to do but sell the bank. Not only does the Breakthrough Banking Blueprint lay out how you can literally reverse this pattern to a point where you will generate industry-leading margins and maximize stakeholder value, the concepts contained in this book are also timeless."

-Adam Mustafa CEO and Co-Founder, Invictus Group

## IMPLEMENT WHAT YOU LEARN IN THE BOOK TODAY!

The Breakthrough Banking Blueprint Toolkit equips you with the bonus templates, tools, videos, processes, swipefiles and more... so that you can transform your culture, capture core deposits, increase loan demand, gain premium pricing and emerge stronger.

**Head to https://EmmerichFinancial.com/bbtoolkit**

CIP Page The Breakthrough Banking Blueprint


Bloomington, MN 55439



Leadership Avenue Press, LLC offers excellent discounts on this book when ordered in quantity for bulk purchases or special sales. For more information, please contact 1-952-737-6730

ISBN: 978-1-890965-11-2
Library of Congress Control Number: 2020913623

Front cover image by: PrimeConcepts.com
Book design by: PrimeConcepts.com

Printed by Leadership Avenue Press, LLC, in the United States of America

First edition August 2020

# BREAKTHROUGH BANKING BLUEPRINT

The "Franchise" System to Get to Top-of-Peer Performance and Stay There

ROXANNE EMMERICH

# CONTENTS

# ACKNOWLEDGEMENTS

*"When you drink the water, remember the well."*
BRUCE SPRINGSTEEN

As I review this book prior to going to print, I have goosebumps. I have an inner knowing that this book will save many community banks, and thus, the communities they serve will be saved from small businesses folding up and the brain drain that happens when the last community bank is eliminated from a community. I truly believe this book can change the world for the better.

If I had to do this alone, I would have created a tenth of the results. The reason this book and its research can help is because of the insights and effort of an army of tireless bankers, friends, colleagues, and family members.

Family comes first.

A special thank you to my husband, David, who tolerates my never-ending quest to understand how to transform performance and cultures at an ever-bigger level and who questions my premises constantly—and sometimes annoyingly (I love him anyway)—to make sure they are solid. It takes a special man to be willing to share his wife with a quest— a passion of the soul that is both my work and my hobby. He informed me without prompting when he met me: "I'll never get in the way of your work—you have a gift you must bring to the world." I'm very aware that not every partner would be that open to sharing me, with all the sacrifices it took. Thank you for tolerating the millions of Delta miles and Marriott stays—I'm sure that was not easy for you. You are the only father I know who somehow managed to be a great CEO by day, do laundry by night, and take sole responsibility for the kids while I traveled. And you're funnier than any comedian I've ever heard.

Our children Casey, Julia, Brandon, Sue, Stephanie, and Spencer have brought great joy to our lives. We could not be happier to see you grow into amazing contributors to the world that are unstoppable, brilliant, and heart-centered.

There are hundreds of clients whom I've been humbled to serve over my decades of research; it would be impossible to list them all. I've had the chance to A/B-test different theories to see how each adaptation of a franchise system would work best to get them to top five percent performance and keep them there. I took that honor to serve you seriously, and now hundreds of banks and their customers will benefit from our research and work. Your openness to take already high-functioning banks and challenge the status quo in pursuit of a dream of an even-better bank has moved me. I appreciate your humility and your commitment to excellence.

I'd like to give a special thanks to two legends of banking who trusted me while I cut my teeth on my "intuitive hits" when I was just a kid with a dream: Al Tubbs, then president of the American Bankers Association while running a bank in Iowa; and Clarence Jones, then president of the Idaho Bankers Association while running a bank with epic performance. They were two of my raving fans when we were just beginning to build the bank performance franchise systems—they believed in the dream while it was still in its infancy and trusted in me to serve them. It takes great humility for a banker who is already achieving a 23 percent ROE to still think we could help them do better—I was flattered and honored.

And I'm grateful that it worked!

I'd like to thank all of our clients, who always trust that what we are doing to make them better would work. It could not possibly have been more rewarding to see so many of you recognized as best places to work and to move to top tier performance and stay there.

I'd also like to acknowledge all the members of my team, who all had a special hand in allowing this book to be birthed. Although I can't list all of you, know that you've all been instrumental. A special thank you goes out to those most intricately involved on this journey, including Terry Slattery, Shaun Heuerman, Kristi Miller, Megan Furth, Melissa Gaines, Adrienne Glusman, Ron Beilin, Steve Gordon, Dianna Booher, Dr. Dale McGowen, Charles Kozierok, Lisa Browder, Misty Allen, and Ford Saeks. Without you, this wouldn't have come to fruition. It's been a blast.

And now I thank you, my reader. I wrote this to create your legacy. I want your journey of a banking career or bank owner or board member to be easier and more profitable. But most of all, I want for you to move swiftly to unparalleled success so you can then take the most important journey of all—from success to significance. I believe community banking exists to help communities thrive and to bring abundance consciousness to their customers—a rising tide lifts all boats. Through your enhanced success, you help others succeed. We must always remember why we exist.

# INTRODUCTION

*"There's a way to do it better—find it."*
THOMAS EDISON

"If I didn't have a kid that's still in high school, I would quit this job." The CEO of a billion-dollar bank muttered this comment during the CEO peer exchange the afternoon before I keynoted the American Bankers Association Community Bankers Conference during the last recession.

I was incredulous. Yes, no doubt the regulators were breathing down this guy's back. Yes, he probably had some classified assets that were going to cause credit losses, taking away any chance of achieving a decent profit for the year. Yes, every day he probably faced overwhelming challenges.

But to this day, those words still ring in my head.

I almost certainly didn't make his Christmas card list that year after I brought up his statement during my keynote the next morning. Imagine how it felt to be one of his team members. Or one of his clients. Or to be him.

He had lost himself. Although he was probably a good person, he certainly created an inevitable result—the loss of yet one more community bank.

## WHY DO SOME BANKS EMERGE STRONG AND MAKE FORTUNES DURING RECESSIONS?

The month following that comment and keynote, I was hosting a seminar where we help banks understand the basic mechanics of how to break through to high performance. On one of our breaks, our executives were high-fiving, smiling, and chattering about an aggressive learning plan to emerge stronger from the recession. One attendee, a man in his 70s, told me he'd been the CEO of four turnaround banks during his career. His "take" on our conference: "I've learned more in two days than in all my 30 years of attending seminars as a bank CEO."

To say that our program was intense is an understatement. As a result, most of the banks in the room were thriving and pulling ahead even though they certainly had some messes to clean up due to the then-current economic disaster.

Later in the day, both our group and the group of bank CEOs meeting down the hall took a break at the same time. As our people buzzed with excitement and enjoyed each other's company in the Minneapolis Marriott that day, they couldn't help but notice the bankers down the hallway. Returning to our meeting room after the break, our bankers commented on the contrast they'd observed in the crowd huddled nearby: slouched postures, frowns, and gloomy dispositions. With pasty white, grim faces, each seemed to be teetering on the brink of bad health.

To top off the scene, one of my team members came to me quite distraught, saying: "Hey, some of the bankers from the other conference are coming into our room and stealing the books off the back table. What should we do?"

"Hmmm." I pondered. "I think it's perfect. Just let it go.

Obviously, they must really need those books."

Since that day, I've watched 13,000 of those community banks be gobbled up. So, this current economic crisis is the perfect time for this new book to be published. Without it, I truly believe we'd watch at least another thousand—or maybe two thousand or more—community banks disappear.

Many CEOs are good bankers with bad systems. They simply can't withstand the pressure of an economy that tanks. And the moves by desperate competitors inevitably compound their struggle to get through a recession.

However, the bigger issue is this: When community banks disappear, communities find that their small businesses leave or fail, and the brain drain begins all around them. When the last bank leaves a community, the community dwindles away. And if too many small communities shrivel and die, America suffers irreparably.

So, saving our community banks in good times and bad is a just cause. Doing this has been my mission for the past few decades as our firm has specialized in helping banks achieve results they never dreamed possible. Community banking is the backbone of our society. Good bankers are good friends—leaders who transform the financial lives of their customers.

Community banks must survive if our nation is to survive.

## THE NEW GAME OF BANKING

Transactional banking is over—transformational bankers are the only ones that will survive the next five years. That new breed of transformational bankers demonstrates wisdom and skillsets far, far beyond what most bankers think possible to achieve within their teams.

During the last recession, one bank CEO referred to me as "a one-woman economic recovery program." Although somewhat embarrassed by the praise, I'll humbly claim that epithet because many CEOs have told my team that they can't imagine how they would have made it through the last recession without us. I was, quite frankly, like a bulldog standing by them and not buying their excuses of what they couldn't do. In fact, they had to figure out how to attract more revenue, more *profitable* revenue, and *safer* revenue. As I stated in my first book for the banking industry, *Profit-Growth Banking*, profit, growth and safety together is the only formula that allows banks to emerge stronger. Safe, *profitable* revenue solves all problems.

Community banking has been my life's work—helping banks achieve performance they've never dreamed possible.

**Cost-cutting is not the answer.** You can't cost-cut your way through a tough recession. Granted, cost-cutting may help you *survive* a short-lived recession; but if you intend to emerge stronger after challenging economic times, you need different strategies with better execution.

Emerging stronger is the game. A small group of banks in this country will pull so far ahead during the next recession that competitors won't be able to touch them. The history books have proven that fortunes are made during recessions.

During the last recession, after a quick-but-remarkable transformation of their results, one banker told me that the executive team had engaged us as their "last ditch effort." As we were moving through the transformation process with them, they shared this comment: "If you hadn't helped us create a fast turnaround, we would've had to sell the bank."

Fast forward to the beginning of this new recession: They are now one of the 10 most profitable banks in the country. And they're still hungry to learn and make their franchise systems even stronger. They push to grow and develop every single day.

Still another bank previously considered themselves a "cultural train wreck." But after using our Thank God It's Monday!™ culture system, they are consistently voted one of the top five places to work in their state.

The list goes on, but the point is simple: Most community banks are subject to the twists and turns of the economy because they do not have the right systems in place or the right skills to implement those franchise systems.

Having spoken at hundreds of bank CEO conferences and taught at several graduate schools of banking programs, I've met many well-meaning authority figures teaching things that are just...plain...wrong. In fact, during your executive education simulations, you may have heard some of these myths yourself:

- "The way to get more deposits is to advertise rate in the paper." False: That's true only if you want hot money that's expensive.
- "If you want to increase your NIM, it means you're taking more loan risk." False: That's more loan risk *only* if you don't know how to attract the best-quality credits and position yourself as a category of one whereby price is a small factor in the decision-making process.
- "The number of new accounts is a meaningful metric." False: That's true only if you don't care about profits. Fully 87 percent of those new accounts are typically unprofitable for the average bank.

These false assumptions and "rules of thumb"—along with many others—are why most banks work tirelessly to be good at what they do but remain far below their potential.

## DESPERATE SOLUTIONS THAT SOUND LIKE GOOD IDEAS—BUT AREN'T

The stories from dozens of bank CEOs every month all align regarding the dangers of the "*solutions du jour*":

### Pseudo Solution #1: Alignment

Alignment companies designed for the manufacturing industry come in to teach bankers how to align to KPIs. While it's a great idea conceptually, those KPIs are aligned to the wrong metrics. Plus, there's no understanding of how to achieve those KPIs, . . . no understanding of what leading indicators drive those lagging indicators, . . . and finally, no integrated systems to drive radical improvement in the leading and lagging KPIs. After such "alignment" attempts, a bank's lack of progress simply becomes more visible—while the bills for those attempts at improvement keep coming in.

### Pseudo Solution #2: Sales Training

Sales training companies dance in and out of banks—most leaving more carnage than results. It is an abysmal failure more than 95 percent of the time.

### Pseudo Solution #3: Branding Upgrades

Branding firms come in and waste the time of many people. When they leave, their deliverables are a few logos that could be bought on freelance websites for under $1,000 and a differentiation slogan like "we close loans within 24 hours." Sadly, hundreds of thousands were flushed with a negative ROI on those dollars.

### Pseudo Solution #4: Staff Changes

New CLOs and SVPs of Retail get hired to replace nonperformers—only to soon hit the unemployment line themselves. One person simply can't change the culture and profitability picture without the right resources and integrated systems and aligned executive team to support the effort.

### Pseudo Solution #5: Marketing Agencies

Marketing agencies consume substantial resources. Almost without exception, they create a negative ROI from their marketing dollars because they don't know what needles to move or how to move them.

### Pseudo Solution #6: New Technology

New CRMs are purchased with great hope that the software will increase sales. Executives brag about their new technology and the expected results. Again, unfortunately, those increased sales never happen.

### Pseudo Solution #7: Special Deposit Programs

Special deposit programs designed to attract more deposits increase the cost of funds. While expensive, such programs do little to attract low-cost deposits that capture the entire relationship. That is what is needed to create ROI from the dollars "invested."

### Pseudo Solution #8: Leadership Training

Military officers come in to teach leadership. Leadership training sure sounds like a good idea. However, the command-and-control model doesn't sell well to teams who don't want to be commanded and controlled. People today instead want to be inspired to be purposeful in and good at their work. Culture survey scores go down. Performance struggles.

**Bottom line:** These ineffective and disjointed programs have no "intentional congruence"—the ability of integrated systems to work together to create a predictable success machine. CEOs report that they've tried these pseudo solutions, and they didn't work. What they don't know is that almost every bank has that same level of failure because what is being sold to them can't possibly work.

Bankers who roll out these and other "new programs" aren't at fault for these failed attempts. After all, they're searching for help and these all *sound* like good ideas. Who isn't for apple pie and motherhood?

The pay-to-play programming offered at bank conferences, where these vendors bought their way onto a stage, make them seem "endorsed" and therefore credible. These vendors are all good people; it's just that their systems, by themselves, aren't enough to create a sustainable positive impact on safety, growth, and profit—at the same time. And that IS the game.

Even if any of these did work, without the *integration* of proven systems of strategy, culture, marketing, sales, service execution, and more, these programs become another distraction instead of a sustainable, breakthrough system.

## YOUR BANK AS A FRANCHISE SYSTEM

When I started this business, I had the great honor to be the primary educator of the leaders of what was voted the top franchise in the country every year I worked with them. At the time, I was an adjunct faculty member at the University of Wisconsin Management Institute, where I taught leadership, management, and board development.

But what I received from the franchise far exceeded what they received from me. I learned the value of building a franchise system that creates predictable success regardless of personalities.

To be more specific: I learned the value of finding the single best way to do everything in a business *and* make sure that every one of those pieces fits together like pieces of a puzzle. In such franchises, everyone and everything aligns in a system of simple steps that can be managed with precision.

Nobody in my banking network had any idea about how to do that, nor had they given it much thought, but I was enamored with the franchise model.

After 30 years of A-B split testing, we have discovered the best systems in banking:

- The best way to find new predictably profitable customers
- The best way to align each person in the bank to the strategic plan every week
- What visibility systems drive the biggest performance breakthroughs
- The best way to teach people to systematically win seven-figure checking accounts
- How best to tie every person to profit on a daily, weekly, monthly, and quarterly basis

These represent just a few of the franchise systems tested to create the most reliable results. Consequently, our proprietary software, cNote, gave each bank the visibility to track performance with their own definition of utopia, along with the metrics and proven systems necessary to support achieving that utopia.

Numerous bank executives using the franchise system say: "Our performance is beyond what we ever dreamed possible." *That* is what a franchise system does.

Southwest Airlines somehow managed to experience over three decades without having a down quarter—even after 9/11. At the same time, the rest of the airlines had a "bankruptcy rhythm" every 5-7 years. When my friend, the past CEO of Southwest Airlines, spoke at our Best Banks in America™ Super Conference a few years ago, he shared the importance of two things: the right strategies implemented correctly and tying them to the right culture.

Those two principles are the cornerstone of the Breakthrough Banking Blueprint™ system.

## FIGHTING THE DRAG

While most banks have several key executives ready to transform them, these passionate leaders are often held hostage by one or two executives who hijack the team's potential. Often those strong executives who are up to the game of transforming their banks don't know how to handle those one or two executives who don't want to play full on.

Let's say the executive team determines that their bank can bring an extra $3 million to the bottom line by improving NIM, an extra $2.5 million by creating a culture that ties people to profit, and an extra $3.5 million by attracting more low-cost core deposits. Those otherwise-adept leaders will let one or two people hijack that revenue potential for the entire team!

Nobody seems to know how to confront the naysayers about how many months they should be allowed to execute their own plan to bring in that $9 million. Sadly, these naysayers are never challenged—and the shareholders suffer. Nobody asks them to cough up their own plan to bring in that $9 million and to trend against progress lines, so that your bank has a fairly good chance of collecting that additional profit. This atrocity of an excellent executive team being held hostage by one or two "wet blanket" executives happens in banks every single day.

You may want to visit our website for case studies of bank CEOs that we've had the honor of serving, so you can read their transformation stories. When I ask them why they didn't ask for our help sooner, there's always a long silence, followed by this common confession: "I thought we should be able to do it ourselves. But now that I know how extensive this franchise system is and what we would have needed to figure out, and how many different resources we would have needed to compile and align, there's no possibility we could have done it on our own."

As a board member or executive team member, can you afford not to take the journey from transactional to transformational bankers? Can you afford not to become a category of one, so you can stop matching rates? Will you survive the next recession if you don't build a predictable, successful franchise system?

Listen to your heart. What is truly possible for you if you ran your bank at its full potential?

You'll find the "breakthrough blueprint" as you read ahead...

CHAPTER ONE

# FROM TRANSACTIONAL TO TRANSFORMATIONAL LEADERSHIP: HOW GREAT BANKS CULTIVATE EXTRAORDINARY LEADERS

*"A time comes when you need to stop waiting for the man you want to become and start being the man you want to be."*

BRUCE SPRINGSTEEN

Buckminster Fuller said that we are poised on the precipice of either utopia or oblivion. He called on us to make a conscious choice to tip the balance to the positive.

In the B-C-D model of life, B is for birth, D is for death and C—what lies between birth and death, is choice. The quality of our choices will determine the quality of our lives.

We all know at a deep, unconscious level that we are challenged to step up to what Joseph Campbell called "The Hero's Journey."

It is hard to deny that we are inspired when we watch others take the choice of the Hero's Journey. When Luke Skywalker discovers The Force is within him. When Harry Potter learns that he is capable of magic. Or when King Arthur discovers that he has all he needs within him to pull the sword from the stone. Myths and stories like these evoke great meaning for us because they prompt a calling. We, too, might have far more power to impact the world than we ever thought possible.

As banks grow from $200 million to $500 million or from $2

billion to $5 billion and then $20 billion, executives who hold their positions and grow with their banks have one thing in common: They accept the calling. They take the transformational journey to hone their skills and ways of "being." They tap into a courage that enables them to discover what they're capable of creating. They make a conscious choice to suspend limiting disbelief.

Alternatively, some executives unconsciously fight to hold on to their limiting beliefs. "We have to have the best price, or we'll lose the deal." "We will have a bad year because the economy is bad." "It's hard to find good people." These are all beliefs that, when believed to be true, produce an inevitable result: limited performance.

As executives sit around tables in the fall each year to craft their strategic plans for the next year, it becomes obvious who is stepping courageously into the future on "the journey" and who is about to be left behind in a small-minded, excuse-filled acceptance of mediocrity and limited beliefs. For many, good enough is good enough.

## ENLIGHTENED LEADERSHIP: BE, DO, HAVE

Enlightened leaders have a unique worldview. Epictetus, the Greek philosopher, said it well: "First say to yourself what you would be; and then do what you have to do."

That observation brings to mind an extraordinary event from my childhood. I remember the warmth of the sun on my left cheek and exactly where the sun was in the sky that morning as I stood with the men at the feed mill surrounding the auger when the corn was dumped in to be ground for the dairy cattle.

No one could deny I was a "daddy's girl." I adored my father and loved working with him in the barn and in the field and going everywhere with him. On our dairy farm we worked tirelessly seven days a week and often from before sun-up to sundown.

One of the highlights of each week was our trip together to

the feed mill to grind the corn for the milk cows. He would drive the truck, while I shifted the stick shift with my left hand when he engaged the clutch. That maneuver was one of our favorite playful bonding moments each week. I felt like a "big girl."

I remember one day at the mill explicitly. Since I was the only kid—and noticeably the only female—at the mill, what was strange became normal. In fact, all of the farmers saw me as "one of the boys" and made room for me in their conversations. (I guess it's no accident that later in life I chose to earn a bachelor's degree in agriculture.) That special day, as we stood around the roller bars that the corn would go through to be ground, they all commiserated about the deep recession happening at that time in the dairy industry, causing neighbor after neighbor to have "sales." What wasn't comprehensible to me at 10 years of age was that these were foreclosure sales.

But there was one significant moment on this particular day when the guy with the ruddy complexion and a slur asked in an exasperated and desperate voice: "When is the government ever going to step in and help us?"

At age 10, I didn't really comprehend who or what this "government" thing was… But as the sun hit my cheek, I had a profound and life-directing insight. I thought: "Why don't grownups just do something different when what they're doing isn't working?"

That was the moment that forever changed me and set my life purpose. It was the moment that defined me. It was when I first understood my soul's code: helping people break out of what is the most attractive of destructive archetypes: the "victim."

A victim is always at risk for what outside circumstances create. Alternatively, those who are "at cause" create results regardless of the economy, limited resources, and what desperate competitors are doing.

A **victim** is oriented to the pattern of "have–do–be." Their language pattern is: "When I *have* enough resources, time, and people and the economic winds at my back, then I'll *do* the things that will allow me to *have* success. If I had the right economy, people, sales training, products, and market conditions, I'd certainly be as successful as those top peers, but I don't *have*, so I can't *be* successful." Victims are always waiting for externals to change before they can create success.

Unlike the victim, the ***worker*** has a worldview based on the pattern "do–have–be." Their mental model is this: "The more I *do*, the more I'll *have*. The more I *have*, the more successful I'll *be*. There's a significant problem with this because, as we all know, the more we do, the more there's still left to be done. And if I define myself by what I do, busy turns into tired, and tired turns into exhausted. Sadly, the more I have, the more there is to lose, so I work harder not to lose what I have!

The ***victor*** instead lives with the approach of "be–do–have." The victor starts with the question: "What kind of person would I need to *be* to *have* the kind of outcomes I want?" The state of "being" takes care of "doing," which in turn takes care of "having."

Enlightened bankers adopt this third worldview: BE–DO–HAVE.

## AN OBSESSION WITH MASTERY

As a banker, is "good enough" really good enough? If you can get your team to build enough trust with customers to master five cross-sales, so each customer knows they don't need to go to other banks to have their financial needs met, is that good enough? Might you move to a level of mastery, so that your team is well over seven cross-sales?

If your close rate on your top 100 most profitable next customers is 50 percent, what would you have to do to close more than 85 percent of your deals (the norm among the highest-performing banks) without matching rates?

When we let go of the egotistical need for applause for accomplishing what is good and instead become constant seekers of our highest potential, a whole new world of opportunity presents itself. Commitment to mastery flows in the veins of those who continue to demonstrate that they're capable executives at an even higher level.

Imagine explaining to Jeff Bezos or Elon Musk that you can't get a 5.0 NIM and a seven cross-sales ratio on new customers or raise your non-interest-bearing deposits to 70 percent of total deposits from 30 percent within a few years. They would fire you on the spot and achieve those goals in a matter of 12-24 months. *That* is mastery obsession—unearthing whatever skills are necessary to make the impossible possible.

When you meet bank executives who rave about what a good year they've had, you may do well to short their stock. High-performing CEOs are often celebratory of their breakthroughs—but *never* happy. They always know there is the next frontier and they are called to pursue it. Most of our member clients are already high performers when they start with us. They are committed to mastery.

## ABUNDANCE CONSCIOUSNESS

Carol Dweck, author of *Mindset: The New Psychology of Success*, writes: "In a growth mindset, people believe that their most basic abilities can be developed through dedication and hard work. Brains and talent are just the starting point. This view creates a love of learning and a resilience essential for great accomplishment."

Abundance applies not only to money, customers, and opportunities, but also to time. A scarcity thinker will be quick to tell you that they can't do something because "they don't have enough time." Time is the great leveler: We all have 24 hours in a day and seven days a week. So, to say you don't have enough time to accomplish X is a clear indication of scarcity thinking.

Our results can never exceed our limiting beliefs. If we think we can't, we can always arrange the universe so we can be right about our limitations. People typically fight hard to defend their limitations as real. Abundance thinkers, on the other hand, find ways to achieve more regardless of the circumstances.

Notice the plethora of banks struggling to achieve even a 4.0 NIM. They'll have at least one executive who speaks with great authority that it "can't be done." They believe net interest margin compression is real. And, of course, they are right. *They* can't do it. But others around the limited thinker can, if negative thinkers stop contaminating them with their scarcity mindsets.

Stand clear of thinking like "we can't get premium pricing because our competitors are tough." Stay away from those who don't believe you can quickly and systematically attract the very best deposits in your market. The only reason you can't accomplish these and other breakthroughs is that you don't seek and apply proven business systems.

Those visionaries who think the "impossible" is possible will create and execute the strategies that make it happen. They will be the leaders of the future.

## DARING LEADERSHIP

C. R. Snyder says that hope is not a warm fuzzy feeling. It is a cognitive emotional process that has three parts: goal, pathway, and agency.

The goal is easy: figuring out where we want to go. The pathway is how to get there, whether that involves a linear plan or an ability to adjust plans with the persistence to move ahead regardless of setbacks. Finally, agency is the belief in our ability to "stay the course." While it is easy for cynics to deliver low blows and poke fun at leaders who believe that so much more is possible, agency is what keeps the leader focused, hopeful, and committed despite those without vision.

Imagine Kennedy, Gandhi, or Martin Luther King Jr. saying: "Oh, maybe you're right. There seem to be so many of you disbelievers. I quit."

## THE INTEGRITY OF YOUR WORD

People make implied contracts all day, every day. If someone suggests a goal and others do not negotiate that goal, then there is an implied contract. For example, coming to work at 8 a.m. is an implied contract. Getting that report done every week by Thursday at 2 p.m. is an implied contract. In other words, if someone asked for something and you didn't negotiate, you then have an implied contract.

Great leaders stand by their word. They do what they say they're going to do. They hit their numbers regardless of circumstances. They hit their deadlines because they said they would. These authentic communicators not only hold others accountable, they hold themselves accountable.

While no person can be 100 percent in integrity with their word, those who are extremely conscious of and devoted to their commitments stand out as true leaders.

The leaders who play the New Game of Banking have made the journey from head to heart. They know that "enrolling" the hearts, minds, and spirits of their teams to accomplish results they never dreamed possible is not only fulfilling, but of extreme service to the world.

Their end game is not success, but significance.

To help you get your entire executive team focused on transformational leadership, I've recorded a video that I recommend you watch together with your entire executive team. It will help each executive understand how to apply the ideas of transformational leadership to their daily interactions with your team.

Get instant access to the video at
**https://EmmerichFinancial.com/bbtoolkit**

CHAPTER TWO

# HOW THE MOST PROFITABLE BANKS "OBSESS" OVER THEIR TOP 100 PROSPECTS

*"You don't get results by focusing on results. You get results by focusing on the actions that produce results."*

MIKE HAWKINS

The average bank in America with under $2 billion in assets garners approximately 40-150 percent of its profits from its top 100 customers. Given that fact, it's a good idea to put identifying and acquiring another 100 just like them above all other strategies. If you do, your headcount won't go up, your operating costs won't go up, and you won't eat up your capital with an acquisition or new buildings. But you could double your profits.

The magic of methodically identifying and closing your top 100 next best customers is that you double your profit while you take on less risk and avoid consuming more of your capital or putting it at risk. Ask yourself this question: What other options do you have that can double your profits with no capital outlay or additional risk?

Of course, setting this as a strategy and executing on the strategy are two entirely different things. Before you can identify and bring on your next 100 most profitable clients, you'll need to solve several problems.

## THREE PROBLEMS TO SOLVE

First, most banks don't know how to identify these prospects because they don't understand the psychographics and firmographics of their *current* most profitable clients. Neither do they know how to find the list of those who look just like their current most profitable clients. Most still focus on old-school demographic marketing with no hope of that working to acquire their next top 100 prospects. Using demographics in marketing for a community bank today can be likened to pulling out a flip phone in a world of smart phones.

Second, even if they do know how to find their next top prospects, they don't know how to systematically and predictably turn them from happy-with-my-current-bank prospects to ecstatic new customers who switched while paying premium pricing. Most banks are not skilled at building reputational equity and differentiation that would pull a low-risk, high-profit account away from an incumbent bank. That requires a special skill set far beyond what most marketing or salespeople in banks have. After all, those incumbent banks probably take reasonably good care of their valued customers, so you can expect the prospect to tell you that they are happy with their current bank. Most bank officers are stalled with that remark and the deal dies there.

Third, even if you solve the first two problems, most bankers don't effectively follow the right system that would close 85 percent (or more) of their Top 100 Prospect List while reaping premium pricing. That's especially true when the incumbent bank is probably priced lower for less risk. To achieve a closure rate of over 85 percent on those prospects who have had a first appointment is essential: You don't want to burn through your best prospects because there are only...well...100 top 100 prospects. Even a close rate of 60 percent is disastrous. You can't possibly double your profits without taking more risk or risking more capital unless you are masterful at not only closing these customers at premium pricing but also securing their entire relationship at the time of opening the first account.

If you haven't been able to figure out those first three steps to systematically acquiring your 100 next most profitable customers, you're not alone. Almost every bank does "mass marketing" and "mass selling." In doing that, they spend valuable resources to inevitably bring in more of the vast majority of customers who lose money for their institutions. Eighty-seven percent of bank customers lose money for a typical bank in America today—and you can't make that up on volume.

You don't have to continue to struggle with this conundrum. Hundreds of banks are not only identifying the right next prospects but are managing to one of their most important new KPIs: "number of top 100 prospects closed with premium pricing." Nothing impacts the profit of a bank more than *that* KPI. We've watched banks move from bottom quartile to top quartile in ROA in less than a year by moving that needle substantially.

So how do you start the flywheel turning to systematically attract and secure the very best prospects in your market—all at premium pricing?

Hire more lenders? No, that's a big fail.

Bring in a sales training firm? You already know that doesn't work—and you know the carnage it creates of your culture. You've seen enough other banks fail at this repeatedly to know that it sounds good as a strategy, but it rarely works. In fact, it is usually a train wreck. If you haven't tried it, you've certainly heard the horror stories from colleagues at other banks.

## THE IRON-CLAD SYSTEM PROVEN TO CONVERT TOP 100 PROSPECTS INTO TOP 100 CUSTOMERS

What does work is a system that requires you to implement the specifics of a blueprint precisely.

There is no room for "slop" in the system. One example of "slop" is when a bank pulls together its top 100 list by asking for nominations to the list from lenders. Instead of a next-most-profitable prospect list, the bank has a list of people who inquired recently (usually B or C credit quality at best). They add in the names of the same folks they've been calling on for years. Those prospects may continue to accept free lunches, but if they were going to change banks, they would have done it long ago.

Even if you master all the other steps that must be followed precisely to get an 85 percent close rate, without proper identification of your top 100 prospects, you face enormous challenges. The right sales system followed explicitly with extreme category-of-one differentiation will get you nowhere if you have the wrong prospects. (To use a farming analogy, the best milk machine on a bull still produces nothing because a bull does not have milk.) At best, you'll have a higher-risk loan with limited deposits. It just wasn't a top 100 prospect to begin with, so there is no rabbit to be pulled out of a hat. That's the best you can do. Perhaps you'll secure "premium pricing," but the pricing is not really premium—it is priced up for risk. That's risk pricing—not premium pricing.

Sadly, our industry has not, until now, had adequate software for banks to do this analysis. We are decades behind what other industries have available to analyze their most profitable customers.

No, you don't absolutely need software to make progress on identifying your next-best prospects. You are far better off to do the psychographic and firmographic work following the prescribed process our team offers as a complimentary service. We're happy to help because it's painful to watch banks prevented from achieving what would be possible if they had a fair idea of their prospect list. Most of the current software is weak and overpriced.

Can you increase profit, growth, and safety at the same time?

The additional profit and safety that come from the new accounts associated with your most profitable prospects because they are *legitimately* the most profitable prospects is transformative. Getting this right is essential.

The biggest stumbling block to getting a Top 100 Smarketing™ program started is identifying prospects to put on your list. The quality of your results is directly linked to the quality of your list. We've put together a downloadable report outlining the seven most common mistakes you're likely to make when identifying Top 100 prospects. It will save you weeks of valuable time, and you'll avoid marketing to the wrong people and missing the opportunity to pull in the most profitable new accounts through proper focus.

Download the report at
**https://EmmerichFinancial.com/bbtoolkit**

Once identified, the next stage is to create "reputational equity." Your prospects need to feel that they are in a personal relationship with you, that you "get them," and that it's clear that you're obsessing about adding value to their businesses.

Gone are the days of "officer call programs" with lenders carrying briefcases and asking questions like: "What would it take to earn your business?" Incidentally, that *is* the single worst question a lender can ask.

The next stage is to deploy a team selling approach using the right sales process—one whereby the prospect can identify that the Level 4 Unique Selling Proposition (USP) will add at least 10-20 times more value than the significant premium pricing that you charge over your competitors. Your offer must be irresistible. No goofy old-school sayings that bankers like to use to defend their pricing such as "we have good people" or "we have good service" or "you get *me*."

Of course, many Level 1 USPs are also necessary for a perfectly orchestrated sales process. Every stage of the sales process must meet all conditions of satisfaction, including choosing the right USPs tailored for that particular prospect.

Then comes the need to apply excellence to every stage of the sale. Otherwise, you risk losing the deal. Remember: There are only 100 of these top prospects. No other prospects will bring as much profit as those on your top 100 list IF you do this right.

Warning: If you aren't maintaining an 85 percent close rate, stop calling on these prospects. Wait until you are ready. Every failed attempt means you usually don't get a second chance for another decade to bring in one of the very few prospects in your market that really matter to your future profitability and safety.

If there are only 100 *next best*—and "next best" is the point—then you can't afford to lose more than 15 percent of those in your sales process due to imprecision or an unproven or improperly executed sales process. At that 85 percent closing rate, you know you have the right system and you can be assured that your team is executing it exactly.

Once that system is working well, sit back and watch your peers look on with admiration and a little envy as you master the game of pulling away their very best customers—at premium pricing that surpasses what the competitor charges. How much fun is it to pull away the best customers from competitors? *That* will confuse them! They still think that they must match rates on high-quality prospects. Who knew?

CHAPTER THREE

# EVERYBODY IS IN MARKETING

*"If you have more money than brains you should focus on outbound marketing. If you have more brains than money, you should focus on inbound marketing."*

GUY KAWASAKI

Most bank executives brought up in the lending, retail, or operations part of the bank believe that marketing is some kind of black art. They have no comprehension of marketing, so they turn the job over to a group of people who know little about how banks increase profit and grow.

Sadly, the "experts" they hire often don't understand how to drive net interest margin (NIM), attract higher-quality credits, or get low-cost deposits. In fact, when I spoke at a bank association marketing conference, I asked for a show of hands of those who felt they understood net interest margin and how they could impact it. No hands went up.

Shyness was *not* the reason. They had no idea what NIM was, why it mattered, how it worked, or what they should do to drive it. Yet this NIM metric is arguably one of the most important for their departments.

## WHAT IF YOU DISCOVERED THAT YOU COULD CUT YOUR MARKETING BUDGET BY 80 PERCENT WHILE YOU DRAMATICALLY IMPROVE YOUR MARKETING METRICS?

Recent research by Tom Ferrell proves why traditional marketing isn't working anymore. His research reveals these facts:

- Businesses think 13 percent of their marketing messages are unsolicited. Contrast that opinion with those of consumers, who consider a whopping 85 percent of the marketing messages they receive to be spam.
- Businesses believe 81 percent of their marketing messages are useful. Customers, on the other hand, say that 84 percent of the marketing messages are not even *slightly* useful.
- Businesses believe 75 percent of their communications are personalized. Consumers see it differently: They say only 17 percent feel personal.

Every day, banks promote themselves in ineffective and counterproductive ways that do nothing to motivate today's customers to buy their financial services. Those wasted marketing dollars could be deployed for important strategic initiatives.

This marketing approach must change. The great news is that it can.

Marketing is not a department. You and your marketing team must adopt the mindset that marketing involves a total way of *being*—a mindset that everyone in your bank must adopt and the related actions that everyone in your bank must execute.

## THE PURPOSE OF MARKETING

What works in marketing has changed, yet only a few smart bank executives are mastering the strategic distinctions to drive an effective marketing strategy.

Please don't blame your marketing team for past failures. It's not their fault. They are being given expensive and misguided solutions in almost every course they take or conference they attend.

In today's environment, the purpose of your marketing department is to constantly upgrade the quality of your customers. That means targeting markets to find "A+" prospects and turning them into "A+" customers by getting all their business at premium pricing.

Everything else is "noise"—expensive noise.

After all, your bank doesn't need more *unprofitable* customers. It's not a numbers game—it's a *profit* game.

Take a look at these five ways to get past the most common marketing mistakes in banking. Then plan to implement the solutions smart marketers use to overcome these errors.

## HOW TO OVERCOME FIVE COMMON MARKETING MISTAKES

If your bank is guilty of the mistakes mentioned above, determine to act now to set yourself on the shortest path to both short-term and long-term profits. Rid yourself of unproductive, old-school methods.

### 1. De-Commoditize or Die

Banks of the future that keep their franchises thriving will be characterized in these ways:

- They will have at least a dozen extreme differentiators. These will not be the kind that ad or branding agencies manufacture but REAL, substantive differentiation.

- Their teams will systematically and effectively execute a proven process to sell those differentiators, making them a "category of one."
- Their "world view" will *not* be that higher pricing comes with risk. Instead, they will attract the very highest quality clientele—all with premium pricing. They'll own the entire relationship and drive loyalty for the long term.
- Everyone on their team will know exactly how their activities tie to profit daily. Team members will master the processes to achieve excellent metrics that indicate team members are massively committed to making the lives of customers better. When bankers are transformational, premium pricing and having the entire relationship shows up in metrics because the customers can't imagine life without your bank and its impact in their lives. Metrics aren't a "have to"—they are a "get to."
- They'll protect their "franchise system." That is, every team member will know the best way to complete every revenue function of the bank. That franchise system includes how they identify their next best customers, how they systematically turn prospects into customers with a high close rate, and how they own the entire relationship.

True differentiation and personalized services represent a compelling competitive advantage. By defining your bank's uniqueness with a Level 4 USP, you too can capitalize on this opportunity.

## 2. Understand That NIM Is Your Primary KPI

When 100 percent of a state bank association's "seasoned" marketers, who have been doing their jobs for well over a decade on average, don't know what NIM is, well, let's just say: "It's not the fault of the marketers."

Net interest margin captures the core idea of banks that truly "get it"—those banks that will remain in business for the long term. NIM serves as your leading predictor of profitability, year in and year out. It's what builds your capital for growth or acquisition. It's what builds your capital quickly if you have problem loans. It's your *Steady Eddie*—the backbone of a healthy bank.

Net interest margin is the gift that just keeps giving. It feeds your reserves to protect you from economic downturns. It allows you to predict profitable income without the unpredictability of revenue. It allows you to invest in improving services and developing your team members.

If you and your marketing team don't have solid strategies to get and keep your net interest margin over 4.5, what rabbit will you pull out of your hat during challenging times when you need to cover loan losses?

When the coronavirus hit, within the first two weeks, the stock market dipped 25 percent while community banks dropped 40 percent. The banks hit the hardest were those that didn't have strong NIM. That was no accident: They are seen as being worth less.

### 3. Adopt Smarketing

Sadly, most marketing departments think their most important metrics are "leads" and "number of new accounts." Yet roughly 87 percent of all new customers will be unprofitable to the bank, and most of the leads the marketers count in their metrics simply deliver those unprofitable new accounts filled with more risk.

On top of that scenario we typically add a misguided sales team thinking that total dollars of new business is what matters, rather than profits, safety, and revenue stickiness.

Then, to make marketing matters worse, leads get dropped. The sales department gets little or no support from marketing to bring in the deals.

Thus, the need for *smarketing*: the integration of sales and marketing. The two must align and work together toward the same objective: more high-profit, low-risk accounts closed at a rate of 85 percent or higher, with a high cross-sales ratio of at least 6.

### 4. Stop All Product Pushes

*"Step right this way and grab the 'special of the day'!. . . Bada-bing, bada-boom!"*

Is that what customers want to hear from their bank? The people they come to as a source of insights that will help them retire with financial independence or thrive as a small business?

Every product push screams: "I DON'T UNDERSTAND YOU, AND I DON'T CARE." As evidenced by Tom Ferrell's research, such pushes serve to further alienate your customers and prospects.

Imagine calling a bank for a CD rate only to hear the "specials" instead of having a skilled *transformational* banker who can take you through a conversation of cost versus price and how to manage your entire portfolio for maximum impact—making rate almost irrelevant.

### 5. Stop Wasting Money on Advertising and Branding

Advertising seldom works. The statement is harsh, but it's true.

Here's the typical process that banks go through. They hire an ad agency. The agency comes up with a slogan and marketing collateral. The bank runs the plan. Nothing happens. The agency says, "Just wait, it takes time." And so the bank waits. And waits… And waits… And still nothing.

You'll do no better with promotional mailings. According to the Data and Marketing Association, the open rate for such mailings now averages 4.9 percent. And that's just the open rate—the conversion rate is much lower.

Want more bad news? Image advertising has a negative ROI. Although it often fills an ego need because it can be fun to see the team's photo in the paper, it's hard to justify putting an ego need in the budget.

So, what does work?

You essentially have three main focus areas where you can invest your marketing dollars: prospects, current customers, and employee development.

Unfortunately, most banks spend up to 70 percent of their marketing funds on advertising to *prospects*—the approach that actually produces the lowest ROI of the three choices. They spend very little on existing customers, which is the second-highest ROI opportunity. And worse, they spend virtually *nothing* on teaching team members to create a transformational experience whereby they bring "talkable service," extreme wisdom, and an ability to own the entire relationship without pricing concerns. According to research, that area of least investment by marketing departments is incidentally the area with the highest ROI from a marketing dollar.

To correct this disparity, start by slashing your advertising budget drastically.

While many ad agencies and marketing departments can make "creative" ads and tools, they almost always lack strategic direction and distinctions about how to drive more profitable revenue. They fail to prove ROI from each marketing dollar invested. As a result, those campaigns do a great job of stroking egos yet little to sell financial services to the right audience—all at premium pricing. Worse yet, well-intentioned board members and team members pressure marketing departments to "get something out there," not knowing that the cost of that visibility is extreme and the ROI is extremely negative.

On top of that, many CEOs will offer the rebuttal that the intent of their ad campaign is to build a brand. Good intention... but bad outcome. The required actions to build on that brand can't be done by a branding agency.

What is a brand? Your brand is what customers say about you.

I've spoken at more than 1000 bank CEO conferences and have

routinely asked the same question for decades: "What makes your bank unique?" Just about every CEO has responded with the same answer: "customer service."

There are two glaring problems here. First, "customer service" is not a brand. Second, if more than 95 percent of bank CEOs say that what differentiates them is their level of service, that response gets an "F" in terms of uniqueness.

Branding often is the "snake oil" of marketing. Banks spend ridiculous amounts of money on branding, but nobody knows what it is or how, if ever, it will provide a positive ROI.

Bank CEOs proudly share their excitement about having invested in a branding process. Yet a year later, not a single bank CEO has ever declared: "Did you see what happened? Branding did the trick—we're making money hand over fist since we did that branding process."

Think about it. When was the last time an A+ $5 million credit walked in the front door of your bank and said, "I'd sure like to pay you 100 to 200 basis points more because your logo and billboards look great"?

Those few profitable, low-risk customers come to you only when they believe you're a transformational banker, not a transactional one. Transformational banking means you have a culture whereby your people have taken their service, knowledge, and sales skills to a level at least four times higher than that of competitors.

Prospects become clients when they can't imagine life without your unique selling propositions (USPs) and when "social proof"—testimonials, provable systems, or third-party stamps of approval—says that you can deliver those USPs.

When you get voted a "Best Place to Work" in your state—that's brand.

When you close over $100 million in new loans by having 50 people work from 7 am to 7 pm on the weekend after a new government program becomes available during an economic crisis so small businesses in the area can cover payroll, that's brand. Both are social proof.

Smart marketing is about transforming your bank so much that clients rave about how different you are. They create a buzz in the community about the impact you've had on their investments and businesses.

The result? More high-profit, sticky accounts and more evangelists spreading the good word about YOU.

And not one dollar ever paid to a branding firm to create those remarkable, talkable experiences.

## START INVESTING IN THE *RIGHT* KIND OF MARKETING TO SEE MAJOR RETURNS

As an astute economics professor once said: "The best money you can invest during challenging times is marketing dollars." He's right. But let me add to his sentiment: "The best return from marketing dollars is transforming your team so they're capable of attracting and building relationships with the very best, most desirable customers, winning all their business and attracting all their friends."

Always start your marketing effort based on proven ROI, but first, transform your culture. Engage peoples' hearts and minds to become passionate about being "transformational bankers" who own the entire relationship with every customer.

Yes, this *does* reverse how most banks do things. But remember: Only a blink ago, there were 18,000 banks in the United States. Today, only a fraction remain.

Most of the highest-performing banks in this country who consistently exceed a 2.0 ROA spend virtually nothing on traditional marketing. Instead, they know how to master the transformation of culture so that "tribal" conversations of customers in the community are abuzz. The word gets out quickly that all the most desirable customers should only go to that bank.

A culture that is unstoppable about extreme and talkable service and impact trumps a creative ad every single day.

CHAPTER FOUR

# THE DEPOSIT DEBACLE: WHY MOST BANKS CAN'T ATTRACT THEIR FAIR SHARE

*"It's the people who don't ask questions who remain clueless."*

NEIL DEGRASSE TYSON

I recently attended two different prestigious bank conferences, both of which had sessions on gathering deposits. Because I'm always looking for the next big idea to offer my client banks to keep them at top performance, I hoped to gain new insights from these sessions.

During the deposit session at the first conference, I ran into one of my member bank CEOs. She's done an admirable job of attracting large, low-cost deposits and had, in fact, just secured a $10 million business checking account that week using the process my team at The Emmerich Group had taught her team. After a few minutes of listening to the presentation, she glanced at me with a "you've got to be kidding me" look. Essentially, the only strategy the conference presented was: "Use technology to close accounts faster." Good idea...but not enough and no specifics.

A few weeks later, I attended another conference where the session on deposits was even more painful than the first. Table groups huddled to share their "best ideas" and then "debriefed" that output with the entire group.

- "Offer incentive pay," one bank executive called out to the large group. Others fired up their pens.
- "Advertise CDs for unusual time frames." More writing.
- "Hire a firm that does scheduled checking account mailings for you." They scribbled a third note.
- "Train your bankers to be universal bankers," said another. Heads went down.
- "Get tiered pricing on your money market or checking accounts with debit-card usage required." Still more writing.

I was incredulous. It was clear that they weren't kidding—they really had not yet tried those things to find out they were about to waste more time and throw good money after bad. All these things have been tried for decades with predictably lousy results, almost without exception.

To be fair, there's nothing wrong with the universal banker model. I recommend it. However, in and of itself, it just simply has never had a substantial impact on any bank I've worked with in helping them get more deposits. The other options *can* work too—they just don't tend to pay for the extra time and money invested. They are weak, "old school" options.

## SPARE YOUR BANK ITS NEXT BIG MISTAKE

The Hippocratic oath is often misquoted as "first, do no harm." What it actually says is this: "I will abstain from all intentional wrong-doing and harm." Similarly, we need to apply the intention of the Hippocratic oath in advice about how to get deposits.

Many of the traditional approaches are just plain wrong, wrong, wrong, and wrong. In fact, some are hurtful and, quite frankly, have caused the disappearance of community banks. Most of those community banks failed or were sold due to very preventable mistakes in judgment. In their attempts to "follow the leader," they modeled other banks that weren't proving out positive ROI on their strategies.

Here are some of the deposit "strategies" that low-to-moderate-performing banks repeat—almost always with disappointing results.

## CD SPECIALS

Newspaper or online ads for CD specials attract a certain client: someone willing to invest only for the best price and willing to move their banking for a few basis points. If you're later surprised at what happens when the CD comes up for renewal and the client runs to the most desperate competitor running their own ad at that time, you have a fundamental misunderstanding of basic human behavior: People rarely change their habits. They will predictably do tomorrow exactly what they did today.

Your ad will attract only those who will leave you for a better rate, so you've paid a considerable price for the predictable opportunity to be dumped when it will hurt the most.

Consider the frightening risk that banks will take if they're relying on this strategy when the American Expresses or Charles Schwabs of the world make dramatic offers. At the most inopportune time, those big firms will strategically decide to crush you and beat you while you're down. When you most need funding is exactly when tough competitors most want those same deposits and will decide they need to crush their competitors in the short term to win in the long term. And they have much deeper pockets than you do as a community bank.

## FIRING THE SVP OF RETAIL

The next most common strategy banks deploy when they need to grow deposits faster is to fire the head of retail and replace that poor soul, hoping for a better result. Sadly, that strategy has two downsides: You're temporarily destroying someone's career and setting up the new person to fail. Based on national statistics, that new hire has less than a 15 percent chance of keeping the job for more than a year.

Team members suffer from inertia, making them unwilling and unable to do the right activities. That "stuck" team then decides to slow-walk the new manager. After all, the team doesn't want to make changes—if they did, they would have made them already. They've dug in their heels.

This unfortunate new manager has to confront the same two fundamental issues as the last person: a team that can't or won't engage in successful behaviors and—the even bigger challenge—an executive team with strategies that start and end at "grow deposits." There are no real defined strategies with any chance of working: no integration of new strategies, no advanced education, no interwoven organizational development processes. Nothing. So, the new head of retail quickly sees the future. When the team doesn't hit the numbers, he or she will be next on the chopping block.

## WELL-INTENTIONED INCENTIVE PROGRAMS

But wait! Banks also like to offer incentive programs. The corresponding adage uttered by many a bank CEO without the slightest variation: "The behaviors follow the money." The idea sounds solid, but again, most incentive programs fail to meet expectations and often cause disruption to the culture or the safety of the organization.

Think of it this way: If someone told you "I'll give you a million dollars to run a mile in under four minutes," you'd desire the money. You'd be interested. You might even be compelled to try to compete, depending on how athletically inclined you were. But no matter how motivated, that doesn't mean you'd actually be able to do it.

The problem? Mind is not all that matters, and there's so much more required to run a four-minute mile than just a desire to do it. The discipline for training. The stage-appropriate technique coaching. A supportive diet to optimize the body's abilities. The training schedule with ever-advancing challenges based on readiness. Access to a team of experts as needed. A good physical therapist. A sports psychologist. The list goes on. Excellence always requires a multi-prong approach that addresses each area of potential failure.

Most banks' incentive programs demoralize rather than support people because they simplistically approach the problem with one trick.

The approach goes back to basic organizational development theory about intrinsic rewards versus extrinsic rewards. Extrinsic rewards like money only work minimally and in the short term and only when people are otherwise underpaid. Intrinsic rewards engage the whole person's heart and soul on an ongoing basis—long after the extra money stops producing the necessary change of behavior.

The simplistic approach of "money will change things" misses so many areas of readiness that are necessary. Competencies. Mindsets. Systems to follow that are proven to work. Extreme differentiation to sell. This list also goes on and on.

Repetition of these conventional wisdom "fixes" fails to deliver the necessary results. Sadly, most banks repeat the ideas they hear from "vendor pitches" or buddies talking in the hallways about what they just started (not what is working) instead of challenging themselves to find out what really works to grow deposits.

I've talked with enough bank CEOs and boards to know that the question isn't: "Do you want more low-cost, core deposits?" The question is: "*When* would you like to start winning low-cost, sticky deposits?" It is imperative to increase your franchise value, and most banks lack the competencies, systems, differentiation, mindsets, skillsets, and strategies.

If you're like most of those CEOs and board members, the answer to that "when" question is an emphatic "YESTERDAY!" To get beyond lip service, though, you must embrace mastery of each area of complexity to generate sustainable and ever-advancing growth of core deposits regardless of market and economic conditions. And that requires a proven system that creates a predictable result.

CHAPTER FIVE

# BUILDING A PREDICTABLE "FRANCHISE SYSTEM" FOR LANDING LARGE, LOW-COST DEPOSITS

*"Simplicity is the ultimate sophistication."*

LEONARDO DA VINCI

Jeff Davis, managing director of Mercer Capital's Financial Institution Group, recently spoke at our Deposit Mastery™ Summit. He shared with us that the old-school approach to bank valuation, using multiples of tangible book value, is now being replaced with weighting. That makes deposits king.

## BIG BANKS ARE STEALING YOUR DEPOSITS

In the last few years, the large banks have offered higher rates and taken far more than their fair share of core deposits, causing community banks to lose ground. As a result, smaller banks are in a new kind of pressure cooker: to get and keep low-cost deposits.

That's only going to get harder. Big banks have invested billions in their apps for consumer deposits, which puts community banks one app away from another risk: losing the vast majority of their deposits.

Remember when banks had car loans? That same thing could happen to consumer deposits.

Your options? You can throw in the towel and match rates or run CD specials that skyrocket your cost of funds. Or you can master how to attract low-cost deposits by getting out of the commodity game once and for all.

I recently met with an executive team whose CFO made a comment that still rings in my ears: "Well, of course we have to match the rates—banking *is* a commodity business." He declared it as definitively as many once said "the earth is flat."

## EVERYTHING IS A COMMODITY GAME—UNTIL IT'S NOT

Coffee was a commodity until Starbucks came along, reinvented the category, and started charging not 10 percent more but nearly 10 *times* more. A Lexus 350 ES and a Toyota Camry are roughly the same car, with an extra $1,000 cost-of-goods in upgrades on the Lexus. Yet the Lexus sells at roughly twice the price.

Every smart business must figure out how to move itself out of commodity pricing. Banking is no exception.

## THE "OLD-SCHOOL" DEPOSIT PLAYBOOK IS BROKEN

The conventional wisdom has solutions for attracting deposits:

- Advertise rates in the newspaper or in online outlets.
- Send promotional product mailings.
- Do "sales training."
- Match rates as people walk in the door.

- Create incentives for your team to attract deposits.
- Offer cash management.

If these are your "competitive" strategies as every bank aggressively goes after the same deposits, you'll likely find that the approach no longer works. Each of these strategies fails for its own reasons.

If you also find that these "tried and true" strategies no longer work, it's not your fault. Very few banks seem to know what really works.

## THE FIVE-STEP FRANCHISE SYSTEM FOR DEPOSITS

Despite the challenges, some banks are growing core deposits at a record pace—all with some of the lowest deposit rates. What do they know that you need to discover quickly before it gets too hard to turn the ship around?

First, they understand that it's not based on just one thing. In fact, most "one things"—such as incentive pay, sales training, product mailings, and "specials"—don't work individually or even in combination. In most banks, these are uncoordinated pieces of a puzzle.

The right system builds on the foundation of what really *is* working today: bringing exceptional value so far beyond "great service" that your clients will say they can't afford to be without you. As a result, your complex sales process works with a 90 percent close rate.

To be successful with the deposit attraction franchise system, banks must follow five critical steps.

### Step 1: Identify Highly Desirable Deposit Prospects

When I lived on a lake in Minnesota, I remember complaining to my husband one beautiful morning when we couldn't enjoy the view without losing our privacy: "Gosh, there's a huge lake out there. But the only fishing boats on the entire lake are right off our dock. Why can't they go somewhere else?!"

"Well, honey," my husband responded, "that's where the fish are."

Most banks fish the entire lake instead of anchoring their boats where the fish are. A small group of people who have large deposits consider many things more important than rates. To repeat: This is a small group—but a mighty one.

To identify that critical group of people and businesses, you need a fail-safe system. With certainty and precision, you must identify that group of top 100 prospects using the right data analytics: psychographics and firmographics. Less-successful banks continue to use antiquated demographic analysis.

A handful of bankers who've tried to figure out their psychographics with a firm that "specialized" in psychographics have told me that they've been in meetings weekly for up to 18 months and still don't have the data that *should* have been available to them in 24 hours! As you might guess, many banks are being sold a bill of goods, and that cost of delay is enormous. At best, the outcome is misguided.

### Step 2: Stop Acting Like You're a Commodity

Once you've identified those large deposit accounts, figure out how to put yourself in a category of one. You have to offer extreme value—something that you alone offer. Your value must be compelling enough that those depositors can't afford to stay with a bank, credit union, or mutual fund that pays more.

If you think that can't be done, sadly, you'll be correct. That's highly likely for *you* because you won't do what's necessary to make it work. However, if you're curious enough to wonder how other banks are positioning themselves in a category of one, then it's likely that you can join their ranks.

### Step 3: Create Reputational Excellence

One of the worst mistakes that banks make is the "officer call program." Setting up your officers to look like salespeople destroys their dignity. Instead of professionals to be admired and sought out for their great insights, the "sales" officer makes little or no impact.

Mark Schaefer, one of today's leading marketing minds, put it this way in his book *Marketing Rebellion*: "The most human company wins." And as the late Zig Ziglar routinely said so well in his programs: "The best way to get what you want is to help enough other people get what they want."

By obsessing over how to add extreme value to those on your small targeted prospect hit list, you can truly attract all their business—with rates being only a minor concern to them. If you don't believe it can happen, that only means you haven't discovered how— *yet*. If you remain "committed" to its impossibility, you'll be right, but others are doing it every single day. Ask yourself this: "What if my chief competitor figures this out before I do?"

### Step 4: Build Your "Smarketing" System

Have you done A/B split testing to determine the optimal way to bring in a $5 million business checking account without price being an issue? Do you know exactly how to get the highest close ratio? If not, then learn from those enjoying a close rate of more than 85 percent on prospects who, quite frankly, loved their current banks and weren't looking to make a change.

Those are the only people you want. Why? Because they're the most likely to be loyal once you attract them away from their incumbent banks.

For 85 percent of these prospects to endure the pain of

switching banks, you have to execute your sales system flawlessly. If you're not closing at that 85 percent rate, either you have the wrong system, or your execution is flawed.

If you don't earn the respect of the affluent immediately and get them to switch within a few weeks of first meeting, they'll kick you to the curb for wasting their time and not give you another chance for at least a decade. Remember, there aren't that many highly desirable prospects with large balances who would consider investing funds with you at a lower rate. You can't afford to experiment with this elite group—you need the right system in place from the beginning.

### Step 5: Expect and Inspect 100 Percent Compliance to the "Magnetic Deposit Attraction" System

One young team at a small $200 million bank practiced this system diligently as they were going through the Accredited Banking Professional™ Certification Program. During the program's training phase, each of the candidates for certification is told to "get in the game" and call on prospects using the system, even as they're still learning.

This particular team at the $200 million bank closed $14 million of low-cost deposits in a matter of two months *before* they were certified—closing five of the six deals they called on. Another bank using this system picked up 10 percent of the size of their bank in deposits in only a few short months.

## WE'VE ALWAYS DONE IT THIS WAY

It is not uncommon for people on your team to chant this to the new hires around them: "Hey, kid, don't get too excited. I've been doing this for 30 years and what I do works. Just do what I do." Those people can be extremely disruptive to your chance for meaningful progress.

Those well-intended but ill-advised old-school bankers aren't getting that 85 percent close rate. And worse, those officers continue to match rates on what they do close. So, although their system has "grown their portfolios," it hasn't grown them for maximum safety, premium pricing, and portfolio retention. And those things matter a great deal in growing your franchise value.

Ego is the enemy. Don't let people unwilling to change and follow the system evangelize those ready to execute it successfully. Those stubborn holdouts will hold your entire organization hostage and keep you operating well below your potential.

Double your deposits and decrease your disruptors. Check out our Deposit Master Class Video Series, where we break down the best ways to get 90% of your deposits to come from your Top 100 customers.

Access the videos at **https://EmmerichFinancial.com/bbtoolkit**

CHAPTER SIX

# WHY YOU SHOULDN'T COMPROMISE ON PRICING

*"The single most important decision in evaluating a business is pricing power. If you've got the power to raise prices without losing business to a competitor, you've got a very good business. And if you have to have a prayer session before raising the price by 10 percent, then you've got a terrible business."*

WARREN BUFFETT

The ability to command significant premium pricing for the very best credits while luring depositors away from banks they love is the magic that every successful bank must master.

The dramatic decrease in the number of banks due to consolidations and failures certainly should cause the industry to reflect. We now have fewer than one-third of the number of banks operating just a couple of decades ago. Some call this a "trend line," but trends have a way of becoming the norm.

Those banks that tried to compete on rate have ceased to exist. Or, worse yet, they received their premium pricing because they took on more risk. By definition, that's *not* premium pricing: It's pricing for risk.

Almost every bank executive has the same complaint: Their firms are filled with bankers who insist that premium pricing is impossible and that net interest margin compression is inevitable. And they are right.... based on *their* mountain of evidence.

But might there be another mountain? As marketing guru and

bestselling author Seth Godin says: “Perhaps the reason price is all your customers care about is that you haven’t given them anything else to care about.”

So, how do you create differentiation that makes your competition irrelevant? Sign a $300,000 “branding” contract? No, because the evidence is in: That doesn’t work. Hire more people to “hit the streets?” That hasn’t worked either. Offer incentive pay for premium pricing? Well, that can have some impact, but often by bringing in more risk—not the ultimate result you want.

If you’ve tried these schemes and they’ve failed to help you command premium pricing, you’re not alone. Almost every bank tries one of these three approaches every few years, with the same predictable result.

## BECOME A CATEGORY OF ONE

Remember the Anthony Hopkins line from *The Edge* movie as he was plotting how to kill the bear that was stalking and killing his team members one by one: “What one man can do, another can do.” If some banks have substantially increased their NIM figures while decreasing risks without any “funny business,” it stands to reason that other banks can as well.

Becoming a category of one *is* possible: Elite, results-oriented banks have done it. The real question is *how* to make your bank a “category of one.” A bank where you never again lose a deal based on pricing. Imagine what it would be like if you never heard another team member utter these words: “We can get this deal IF we match the rate.”

## COMPROMISING ON PRICE IS AN ADDICTION

Once started, price-matching can’t be stopped without an extreme intervention—or a profound enlightenment. And the ravages of discounted pricing can cause a debilitating future impact. This addictive behavior:

- Sabotages your ability to recruit, hire, and train the best.
- Deteriorates your capacity to deliver the very best customer service.
- Robs you of the ability to offer the very best top-line products.
- Blunts your release of cutting-edge products and services.
- Encourages your stockholders to accept an offer from a competitive bank that has figured out pricing. And that ultimately destroys your independence.
- It is a slippery slope with a very dark ending. Regulators are ready to pounce on banks that have not figured out how to get and keep low-cost deposits. Unfortunately, most banks are well down that slope already—the only question is whether they can save themselves before it's too late.

The first step to stop the deadly slide: Put aside the "world view" that you must either match rates or lose the business. That's scarcity consciousness.

Enlighten your team. Take them toward abundance consciousness: Instead of competing for pieces of the pie, challenge them to grow the pie. Keep in mind this fundamental, transformative principle: Always give ten times more value than the additional dollars you charge, and people will beat a path to your door.

Discover how to boost your net interest margins with our masterclass video series.

Get instant access at **https://EmmerichFinancial.com/bbtoolkit**

CHAPTER SEVEN

# THE PATH TO PREMIUM PRICING: POWERFUL USPS

*"Only children, fools, and cowards would allow a company to treat them as if prices were set by customers."*

MOKOKOMA MOKHONOANA

Sixty-six something of substantial value that nobody else in your market provides, and make sure your value outweighs the financial impact of your pricing. That's the core of the premium pricing formula.

Quality service, good people, and new offerings, for example, only give you permission to play—they never command premium pricing. For that, you'll need to differentiate yourself with powerful unique selling propositions. (USPs).

## USP DEFINED

A USP is a unique aspect of a product or service that offers an explicit benefit and fulfills a *real* customer need. There are the four levels of USPs:

**Level 1:** These USPs offer basic differentiation. Build these around your competitors' weaknesses or the unmet needs of your target markets.

**Level 2:** These USPs could be the special differentiation of products and services—your cool app, nifty online banking site, or instant-approval mortgage. You need these Level 2 USPs, but they're easy to copy, so the competitive advantage they offer will be short-lived.

**Level 3:** USPs at this level include the special education and certifications you've earned to put you in a league of your own. They differentiate you as the indisputable expert in your market. Banky™ winners often tell us that they garner as much as eight times the growth the first year after receiving that award when they use it properly in the sales process. Such awards and certifications serve as clear marks of distinction—they identify the elite among the elite.

**Level 4:** These strongest USPs are proprietary processes and systems that tell clients you're worth at least 10 times more than the additional amount you charge. Rational people will always pay more for something when they can see a significant ROI. Level 4 USPs allow you to earn a remarkable premium and take you far beyond the commodity world, where desperate competitors survive by matching rates.

## WHERE TO START?

First, ask yourself this: "What matters to my customer?" and "What have my customers not thought of yet that they'll value so much that they'll move to us from a bank they love?" The second step is to rank your list of USPs from most to least important for the customer. Finally, for each USP on the list, brainstorm outrageously dramatic differences.

A powerful USP has to be truly unique; otherwise, it will not motivate buyers to pay premium prices. You need to distinguish your bank from your competitors with a *dramatic* difference, and your customer's opinion about that difference is all that matters. Your USP must address a real customer need in an original way.

Many banks spend hundreds of thousands of dollars with branding companies to receive a differentiator like "we can close your loan within 48 hours." That's nice. Use it. But that's only one differentiator. You better have at least a dozen more that are equally powerful or more so!

## CONSIDER YOUR USPS A TEST

The process of generating USPs is a test to see how well you understand your customers. "We're the biggest" or "we've been in business the longest" are ineffective USPs. Sadly, customers don't care how long you've been in business.

Drill down into what characteristics really satisfy the customer's need. "*We've been in business for 120 years*" says you're not a fly-by-night firm. But who's going to pay 150 basis points more on a loan just because your bank was standing in 1893? Loans-R-Us is perfectly willing to undercut your rate. Sure, you may get a few nostalgia buffs, but don't count on paying the bills by gaining their business.

So, what does a great USP look like? Again, that depends on what your customers want. In addition to the general appeals—like "96 percent of our customers say they would recommend us to a friend," or "fresh, hot pizza in 30 minutes or less"—there are endless clever examples that show solid differentiation in a given market.

You'd think easy-open packages would be a no-brainer USP,

but the company Man Crates engages in macho marketing. They ship "stuff guys like" in wooden crates that have to be opened with a crowbar. The company's Help page even shows a rough graphic of a man's arm holding a crowbar over the words TRY HARDER. That's it—in its entirety. You better believe it costs more to ship goods in a wooden crate than a cardboard shipping box. But Man Crates' customers gladly pay the premium for the clever, hilarious USP.

TOMS Shoes has a different clientele: the socially aware consumer looking to change the world. For every pair of TOMS shoes sold, the company donates one pair to a needy child somewhere in the world. I guarantee customers will pay more for their pair of shoes at TOMS, but they're willing to pay that premium for the USP especially designed to appeal to their altruism.

These are core examples of the kinds of things that work in the consumer market. For commercial clients, you'll need a far more powerful USP if you want to command premium pricing and pull away another bank's best customers.

## PRIORITIZE YOUR USPS

Once you've generated a few dozen ideas, it's time to prioritize them. Find the USPs that matter *most* to your customers, the ones that satisfy the need in a dramatically different way. No, I'm not talking about doggie biscuits at the drive-thru or free placemats with every new checking account. Yours must zero in on meeting REAL needs with ingenuity and creativity.

And once you've found a great USP, don't stop! You don't need just one. In fact, you may need 15-25 total and at least three that are specific to each of your defined target markets. The magic happens when you have many USPs for each psychographically defined target market and when every team member uses these USPs appropriately and judiciously in the sales process.

One of the most difficult tasks for bank executives is to sit in a board room and try to come up with USPs—especially the Level 4 USPs that lead to premium pricing and extreme differentiation. It's the old "Why does Tiger Woods have a swing coach?" question. The answer: "Because he can't see his own backswing."

If you find it challenging to develop your own breakthrough USPs, don't worry. You're not alone—by a long shot. You're just too close to the problem. It helps to have someone who has done it hundreds of times guide you through the process.

How do you know you've latched onto the best USPs? Your customers tell you why they're willing to pay thousands more to have that specific benefit.

## KEEP YOUR USPS FRESH

Once your USPs are in place, don't let them go stale. Desperate competitors will try to replicate your strong USPs. No worries. That's why you have multiple USPs, why you craft each one as a hand-in-glove fit for one or more of your target markets, and why you have a process to keep delivering new ones.

It's the job of the executive team, along with the marketing department and sales managers, to constantly update the USPs to stay miles ahead of the competition. This is NOT a job that executives should delegate.

Remember: The best USPs in the world will do nothing for you unless they are part of a great sales process designed to capture premium pricing.

## NURTURE PROSPECTS THROUGH A PREMIUM PRICING SALES SYSTEM

Having great USPs without a strategic sales process proven to command premium pricing is like having a teen in her prom dress on a Tuesday night: She looks good, but she's not going anywhere.

Most sales training fails to address how to get premium pricing. In fact, that training often disengages the workforce. Thousands of banks have spent millions of dollars on sales training only to lose a third of their people and turn off customers and prospects with what feels disingenuous at worst and unhelpful at best.

At most banks, the salespeople have only begun to tap into their true potential. They just don't have the confidence—much less the proper system—to go after large customers who are happy with their current banks and would be willing to pay premium pricing. If they make a call, they hack away with no clear understanding of the need for the system to be tight and perfected.

But it's not the fault of your salespeople. The problem is that the lenders haven't been told there's a better way to do their jobs. They weren't instructed on how to handle all the other desperate bankers ready to run the papers out for a signature if their lowest bid is accepted.

The right sales system can help your people get excited about (and become far more effective at) pulling in the very best customers without ever hearing price mentioned.

A big focus at each of our Sales and Marketing Bootcamps is to work with you to create your foundational USPs. You and your executive team can leave with your USPs in hand, skipping the endless meetings and avoiding spending hundreds of thousands of dollars to get it done. If you want to take this shortcut, attend the next Bootcamp. For dates and information, go to **EmmerichFinancial.com/events** or call **952-737-6730.**

CHAPTER EIGHT

# HOW NOT TO LOSE MILLIONS WITH YOUR NEXT MERGER OR ACQUISITION

*"I've been through a couple of mergers—they're not that fun. And it is easy to lose your focus on this grandiose mission you established for yourself as an independent company."*

JEREMY STOPPELMAN

What happens to profits after mergers and acquisitions should cause most boards to pause before jumping into one.

Study after study shows that 70 to 90 percent of all acquisitions fail to meet their financial objectives. One recent study found that 83 percent of M&A activity hadn't boosted shareholder returns, while another study concluded that total returns on all M&A turned negative.

Let's be frank: Bank acquisitions are rarely applauded as financial home runs. Some end up as the cause of failure of the acquiring bank. With all this data, it's interesting to note that many banks' strategic plans include intentions to acquire. For many, it will be their demise.

Acquisitions *can* be great, but they work *only* if you have your own "franchise system" of predictable success in place. For it to work, you must drop the acquired firm into your template of profitable and safe revenue systems, along with your cultural systems that tie everyone to profit and the strategic plan.

Whatever your problems, they're magnified after an acquisition. Hard to imagine that your current issues could get worse? They do: With a bigger ship to steer, changing course gets harder.

Have a culture problem? It can and will get worse. Your retail department can't attract the entire relationship? After an acquisition, they'll remain order-takers. Can't get your lenders to stop matching rates? Expect that problem to continue and likely worsen: There will now be more team members matching rates, and they will gang up on your executive team to tell you that "you don't get it—you *have* to match rates."

You'd better know what you're doing far beyond following good legal and financial direction. Almost all mergers and acquisitions are so disruptive to the culture of *both* firms that it can take two or more years after the culture derailment to get sufficiently back on track to attend to the business at hand.

Beyond just hearing the stories of acquisitions and mergers gone bad, you'll want to learn the lessons so that you don't have to *relive the experiences*. Tuition in that school of hard knocks is very high. An acquisition or merger failure can rob millions from your bottom line or even lead to the demise of your organization.

## AVOID THESE SIX PITFALLS OF MERGERS AND ACQUISITIONS

Here are the most common pitfalls that can derail the otherwise bright future of a bank.

### 1. Acquiring for the Wrong Reason

Mergers or acquisitions happen for only two reasons. The first is that you aren't getting the growth and profits you need to keep up with the competition, and you think the acquisition will help solve your growth and efficiency problems. If that's your reason for merging or acquiring, I can almost guarantee that your acquisition or merger will be tough to explain to shareholders a few years later.

Why? Because the very models, systems, mindsets, and skillsets that caused that lack of performance will make for an infinitely worse result when you add the complexity and the cultural challenges of a merger or acquisition. If you couldn't get quality credits at premium pricing *before* an acquisition, don't think that will change when your entire team gets distracted and has yet another excuse to avoid figuring it out.

If you were unable to create a steady stream of enthusiastic, evangelistic, quality clients before the acquisition, consider what will happen when you add the "us-versus-them" anger, excuses, and merger disruption phenomenon. Let's face it: In an acquisition, executives of the acquiring team often feel as though they've gained 10 IQ points and treat the executives of the acquired firm as if they've lost 10 IQ points. Under those circumstances, problems compound.

Unless you have your own house in order, the chance of solving your problems with an acquisition is slim to none. If you've not yet buttoned down your "franchise model"—especially as it applies to profitable revenue and culture survey scores in the top 40 percent —you can count on landing in the bottom quartile of your peer group and remaining there for *years*.

The *only* right reason for a merger or acquisition is to strategically transform your growth prospects—new offerings, new key markets, and so forth—to reinvent your business model. The point of an acquisition is to fundamentally redirect your business strategy. And if you're doing this, please understand what you're getting into and have realistic strategies that make sense.

The key is to have intentional congruence and a plan to create a synergy whereby two plus two equals five. By dropping an institution into an exciting "franchise system" that is working—one whereby you systematically attract the best prospects at premium pricing with the entire relationship and have a culture of "bring it on" that people are excited to step into, the newly acquired people will quickly become disenfranchised. Next, they become disruptive. Following that, your team members who have been with you for decades lose their spirit as "everything feels like a fight." The "we-they" culture fight erodes not only the soul of the organization but the souls of the people in both firms.

All of this is, of course, unacceptable for those serious about their fiduciary responsibility to their stakeholders.

When an acquisition or merger is executed correctly, for strategic reasons and with an enlightened process that respects and grows people while creating an enviable culture, it can help a bank catapult to a level it can't accomplish through organic growth only.

### 2. Misdiagnosing or Underestimating the Financial Risk

Acquisitions whereby the acquired bank is at most 10 percent of the size of the acquiring bank typically do little to increase risk to the core operations or financial stability of the acquiring financial institution. That said, even with a small acquisition, the possibility of a cultural clash that goes on for years can extract massive energy from your team. The time and attention spent on dealing with the "problem child" can take you off course from an otherwise sound strategy.

If the acquisition is greater than 20 percent of the size of the acquiring organization, then batten down the hatches: The risks are real. If you think your primary job is to get operations running smoothly and to convert systems, then you're in for a very costly, unpleasant lesson—one that many executives barely survive with any level of sanity. One bank CEO secretly told me that the two years following his last acquisition were the two worst of his life.

### 3. Scoring No Big Wins in the First 90 Days

In the first three months, you must make customers fall in love with you—not just accept you. Big new deals from that market should fly in the door during this "opportunity" window.

You must win over executives' hearts, minds, and souls. And you must gain managers' commitments to play to win. Your frontline will need to love saying "we" instead of "we/they."

After the first 90 days, the door slams shut and the ugly cultural debacle begins.

Unique selling propositions (USPs) and the service that customers experience in that first 90-day window must compel them to spread the word in your community: "Everybody, move your accounts over here because these bankers 'get it.' "

Here's how it usually goes instead. Executives focus only on getting their core systems aligned as the number one priority. Sure, it's important to not have a core-system integration fail, but system alignment pales in comparison to cultural alignment. You have cultural alignment only when your people know how their roles tie to profit, employees feel revved up about the vision, and the community raves about doing business with you.

Customers make up their minds quickly about whether your merger will be a good thing for them. They need to see immediate evidence of "remarkable" customer service. They must feel excited that this new reality represents a remarkable improvement for *them* in every way. Your USPs must create a buzz in the community that gets everyone in line to become your new customers.

If those customers decide that your merger won't be good for them, they'll run directly into the arms of your competitors. Once they've gone, you'll discover that you've risked your capital to buy the best customers of that acquisition—who have now been picked off. Oops. As Dr. Phil would ask: "How's that working for you?"

The "conventional wisdom" that is often shared from the stage of the Acquire or Be Acquired Conference is that you can assume that you'll lose 30 percent of the customers from the acquired bank. Thirty percent? That's all your profit!

If you're doing things right, you shouldn't lose a single one! In fact, you should also quickly pick up some of the best prospects in that community.

Clearly, you need a plethora of big wins with team members and customers. And yes, this all *has* to happen in the first 90 days.

### 4. No Clear "Easy Button" Franchise Systems

Yes, it's important to look at the tools, systems, and vendors of both organizations and quickly decide which of them you'll use. However, there are other things to figure out quickly when deciding which "franchise system" will work better for you:

- How easily do your quarterly reviews get done *and* tie everyone to profit as well as to the defined values and behaviors of your organization?
- How do you accurately identify your next-best top 100 customers?
- How do you systematically bring in those top 100 prospects at a minimum 85 percent close rate?
- What are the cultural performance systems (daily, weekly, monthly, and quarterly)?
- How are your teams structured, and what process do they follow to systematically pull in 7-figure low-cost sticky deposit accounts?

The acquired employees will expect you to come to them with a solid franchise model, including the following:

- New employee orientation
- New client orientation
- Proven ways to target market niches
- Solid integration between the marketing and sales processes
- Critical drivers for each position in the bank

- Excellent service standards, with specifics on how you measure and improve those leading indicators every single quarter
- A step-by-step sales system, dictating how to optimize sales meetings and coaching sessions consistently in all regions
- Status reporting on key initiatives, critical drivers, KPIs and weekly implementations of the strategic plan to make sure all initiatives and metrics are accomplished, regardless of the competition or the economy
- A system managers need to handle variations from implementation of key metrics or to the weekly alignment to the strategic plan.
- Visibility and celebration systems to keep everyone aligned to your values and outcomes

And the list just goes on.

The bottom line is that you must have your house in order. If you think you'll figure things out after you acquire, I have two questions. First, how many millions of dollars in profit are you willing to forfeit while you figure things out? Second, will you still be standing long enough to produce that kind of miracle?

### 5. Failure to Manage Necessary but Unpopular Actions

Let's be honest here: If the operation you are acquiring had the systems to drive it to the top 10 percent of peers in key metrics, it likely wouldn't have been acquired. While that's not always the case, it's highly likely. So, something has to change.

Perhaps you have bankers loved by customers but with too many poor-quality loans. Maybe they've matched rates on the good loans, forgoing potential profits. Or maybe the acquired executives are unaware of the new game of banking and ill-prepared for it. As a result of these or other issues, they've been unable to produce the necessary results.

Maybe the acquired managers lack the skills or systems to set up key metrics that drive important KPIs. These managers may have been subject to swings in the economy or the competition, so not hitting their numbers became acceptable with a good excuse as a replacement.

### 6. Profit-Crushing Culture Clash

Now for the big issue—the elephant in the room. Culture is cited repeatedly across all industries as the number one reason mergers and acquisitions fail. Remember that long-ago political slogan: "It's the economy, stupid!" The corollary when it comes to an acquisition or a merger: "It's the people!"

Imagine a bring-it-on-and-make-it-happen-no-matter-what bank culture whereby people are passionate about what they do, have fun at work, are used to winning, and allow little space for excuses. Now overlay that picture with customers raving about the care they receive at that bank where they are brand advocates—they can't *imagine* life without you.

I never want to miss getting into a bank within days of an acquisition to "get in their heads." The goal? Massive transformation of mindset to eliminate the potential for the "we/they" story that quashes the souls of people for at least two years and crushes the profit potential of that acquisition.

Nothing trumps culture. Culture trumps sales training. Culture trumps great management. Culture trumps strategy. Culture trumps a great market. Culture is king. And if you don't have a plan to get everyone holding hands and confidently singing *We Are the World*, it may be best to send your lawyers home, no matter how far along you are on the acquisition path.

A transformational culture means that you don't have "middle management breakdown." Managers know how to lead, bring people along, and keep them focused on the executable parts of the strategic plan. And they know how to coach underperformers to either start meeting their metrics or free up their futures for jobs elsewhere that better fit their skillsets.

A winning culture dictates that you execute precisely. Although many people say they don't like to be measured, they'll love to be measured your way in a spirit of fun and with the customers' best interests in mind.

A supportive culture means you aren't losing the typical 37 percent of a manager's day dealing with dysfunctional behaviors and low performance (the current national average).

## AVOID TOXIC, WEAK CULTURES

In a weak culture, there are "agreements." Employees *agree* to whine instead of presenting solutions. They *agree* to gossip as opposed to confronting and improving situations. They *agree* to spew out excuses as a replacement for results. Likewise, managers *agree* that such behaviors are acceptable instead of stepping up to address them. Yes, that's a culture—it's just the wrong kind.

Culture systems need to be integrated with your existing organization as well as the organization you're bringing into the fold. Both need to operate based on healthier agreements.

Leaders must understand that culture isn't a "feeling" but rather a series of interconnected systems which allow a results-rule-bring-it-on attitude combined with the competencies to make remarkable results happen. Those who do not get this cannot create a sustainable culture that rocks.

Here's the good news: Contrary to conventional wisdom, culture transformation doesn't take two years. It can happen in a day. But keeping the new culture alive, advancing, and tied to sustainable profit increases without risk, well, that takes longer than a day.

## CREATE A "THANK GOD, IT'S MONDAY!" CULTURE

Don't even think of doing an acquisition without excellent progress on a plan to transform and transport the culture to a level whereby everyone says in unison: "Thank God, It's Monday! I LOVE my bank!" My *Thank God It's Monday!®* book (thank you for making it a *New York Times* and international bestseller) explains a proprietary system to transform your culture. Many high-performing banks have the entire team read it because they make culture everyone's job.

If you get culture right—and that's a big IF—an acquisition can be a brilliant move. Keep focused, and you can win this challenging game!

CHAPTER NINE

# CREATING A STRATEGIC PLAN THAT DRIVES PERFORMANCE AND PROFIT

*"People in any organization are always attached to the obsolete—the things that should have worked but did not, the things that once were productive and no longer are."*

PETER DRUCKER

According to Mark J. Perry, professor of Economics and Finance at the University of Michigan, only 52 companies have been ranked continuously in the *Fortune 500* since 1955. More than 89 percent of the companies from 1955 have gone bankrupt, merged with or been acquired by other firms, or have fallen from the *Fortune 500* list at least once.

Despite this dismal history, most bank executives will approach their annual strategic planning as if disruption couldn't happen to them. They assume that past success predicts future success. That is naïve and dangerous for their stakeholders, and it will prove heartbreaking for their team members who are passionate about remaining employees of a community bank.

The thinking that your previous success will ensure future success is flawed—especially in an industry in the throes of VUCA: volatility, uncertainty, complexity, and ambiguity. You may have the best of intentions with your strategic planning, but blockchain, cryptocurrency, pandemics, recessions, natural disasters, new apps, and competitors will create disruption. The question to consider is: Will your plan make your bank the disruptor, or will it, by default, become the disrupted? Most fortunes are made during recessions.

A $200 million bank came to our organization with great humility a few years ago—they were in a struggle. The CEO confessed: "If we don't get this turned around, we're going to need to sell." Now, just a few years later, their NIM has increased over 150 basis points while they've significantly strengthened their credit quality. Plus, they've grown more than 30 percent organically—all while dramatically increasing their profit. The CEO recently told me they are now looking at acquisition targets!

The right strategies executed correctly can rapidly change the horizon for a bank that also has the right systems to implement those strategies.

Another bank CEO told me recently: "I belong to a CEO group. There, they always tell me what I need to fix. But they never tell me *how* to fix it." That's a real problem at most banks: the wrong strategies poorly executed.

Many banks struggle repeatedly with the same issues. The problem? Most banks have zero strategies in their "strategic" plans. They fail to create *real* strategies that address issues such NIM compression, attracting low-cost core deposits, and earning the entire relationship. The inability to break through those issues means they have no capacity to tackle the even bigger challenges looming on the horizon.

Sitting in on a strategic planning session offered at a recent national banking conference, I came to understand why so many banks continue to use antiquated strategic planning processes. They simply don't know that the old-school systems that most banks still use are more than just ancient—they are dangerous to the bank's very existence. Most of the strategic planning "authorities" in banking are numbers people—they can crunch the numbers but they can't tell you how to get to the numbers which is the point of strategic planning.

Let's start with the basics: An authentic strategy creates results despite limited resources. If you have the same problem two years in a row, you likely didn't have an authentic strategy but rather a list of things to do. Almost every bank has exactly that in what they call their strategic plan. And if that's the case, it's no accident that the same problems persist year after year.

The antiquated strategic planning process used by over 90 percent of the banks in this country—the ones that aren't pulling ahead—is the norm because even well-intentioned executives are unaware of what the best-performing banks *are* doing. Unfortunately, most banks will unwittingly create a strategic plan for the current year that ensures that they will not exist five years in the future. And that happens regardless of how strong they've been for decades. Past performance is simply no assurance of future success.

Successful banks do not compete on the commodity playing field. Even with the threat of extreme disruption and dark economic forces, there will always be a bright future for transformational, enlightened, ambitious banks.

## THE FIVE BIGGEST STRATEGIC PLANNING MISTAKES AND HOW TO AVOID THEM

I've worked intimately with more than 500 banks, and their CEOs have proudly shared thousands of strategic plans. In these plans, I routinely discover five profit-killing mistakes that crush their potential to be elite, results-oriented banks.

### 1. No Plan That Makes the Competition Irrelevant

"MeToo" is an existential problem that most banks face: their inability to differentiate. Instead, they remain commodities, causing them to be crushed in the competition for deposits and loans. That, in turn, leads to net interest margin compression.

Your plan must be built in every way so that *all* the most profitable customers currently served by your competitors move to your bank. If your plan doesn't have clear strategies to make that happen, it would be smart to sell now before the inevitable.

### 2. A Boring BHAG®

All elements of your plan must align to meet your 10-to-15-year Big Hairy Audacious Goal (BHAG). If your articulation of the BHAG is weak (such as "$1.5 billion with a 2.0 ROA"), you lose the power behind a real BHAG to mobilize the troops around an aspirational vision.

### 3. Stale Plans

If you want a sure investment, short the stock of any bank where an executive says this: "We do strategic planning only once every two years. Besides, we haven't finished the objectives we decided on last year." Either of those two sentences indicates a bank about to spiral downward. Executives who utter both statements are running a bank that won't be around for long.

If a bank isn't doing strategic planning at least annually (I recommend quarterly), it has no chance of adjusting as situations change and no clear "mountain-climb" to the BHAG defined for 15 years into the future. Rarely do I see a sustainably high-performing bank that doesn't have a defined quarterly process, appropriate weekly accountabilities, and the *right* systems to achieve results.

High-performing banks share a common secret: They align their entire plan to the BHAG, target the most profitable markets, and then follow a rigorous process of quarterly adjustments to keep themselves on track for what otherwise seems impossible.

### 4. No Daily, Weekly, Monthly, and Quarterly Alignment

If the meeting rituals and periodic alignments don't allow for all team members to know how their activities tie to profit on a daily, weekly, monthly, and quarterly basis, the chance of high performance is remote.

Everything, everything, everything needs to align to ensure that every KPI, critical driver, key initiative, and outcome is achieved on schedule. Visibility, authenticity, accountability, motivation, and follow-through—all are essential for the plan to work.

There is much talk lately of a new alignment tool that was designed for manufacturing. Many CEOs have confessed that they have the tool now, but it still isn't making a difference because it's not aligned to what banks need.

cNote™ Success Analytics Platform is a project management and alignment tool that helps banks align daily, weekly, monthly and quarterly with the right systems to accomplish their utopian vision and ties to what really matters to drives KPIs. It details every step to increase cross sales, manage the Top 100 process to systematically close Top 100 prospects and the proven strategies that must be managed correctly in order to accomplish aspirational KPIs. With cNote, in less than three years, banks often exceed "utopia" on several metrics as they've defined them. Having the right project plans under ideal conditions, as well as "exception-based reporting," ensures that you stay on track with every key metric and project. In cNote, the optimized project plans are detailed with checklists, conditions of satisfaction, and step-by-step templates, so that you get the benefit of years of split-testing on what really works in high-performing banks. Visibility to outcomes has little value if the right systems to accomplish those outcomes are not managed.

### 5. No Critical Drivers

Many banks feel a sense of satisfaction when they finish their plan and it contains specific KPIs, such as a 2.00 ROA, 17 ROE, efficiency ratio of 52, or asset size of $760 million. However, listing KPIs without understanding the critical leading indicators (by individual and company) that drive the lagging indicators does little for your success. Hitting those numbers will otherwise require pixie dust, magic wands, and a little hocus pocus.

It's meaningless to say that you're going to hit a certain ROA without declaring how many properly defined top 100 prospects you'll bring in at least 100 basis points above your competitors' pricing. Your chance of hitting that ROA will be subject to competitive forces and swings in the economy.

Successful executives drive performance regardless of the market and competitive forces. After all, they promised good people called stockholders, who worked hard for their money, a return on their investment.

A good strategic plan requires supporting stage-appropriate critical drivers *and* the proven strategies with explicit iron-clad plans, combined with the developed competencies, to achieve critical KPIs. A strategic plan is *not* a wish list.

All our clients use a one-page strategic plan along with the implementation process buildout—this plan forces extreme alignment and true strategies. Download that same template plus an audio explanation of how to use it and how to avoid common mistakes at: **https://EmmerichFinancial.com/bbtoolkit**

CHAPTER TEN

# THE MINDSET FOR HIGH-PERFORMANCE ACCOUNTABILITY

*"Stop wearing your wishbone where your backbone ought to be."*

ELIZABETH GILBERT

Mamas love their babies. Bankers love their products and systems. And often, bankers are unwilling to change what they've created because, . . . well, . . . they love their babies—even the ugly ones. But fortunately, your banking success has very little to do with those babies you love and much more to do with *how* you love them.

Ever wonder why the license fees from a patent rarely command more than 1-5 percent of the revenue? The magic of high performance is not in the *what*, but in the *how: how* to differentiate from the commodity business of banking, *how* to execute on the plan, *how* to monetize your differentiation.

And most banks fail miserably at the *how*.

After 30 years of working with many of the top-performing banks in the country, one thing is crystal clear: One of the biggest challenges for any bank CEO is helping their people understand how their individual contributions *really* affect profit on a daily, weekly, monthly, and quarterly basis. Yes, their people stay busy—but busy isn't the end game.

Once they understand what matters most, the next challenge is to get team members to develop the motivation, confidence, and knowledge to *do* those high ROI activities that actually move the needle rather than what they've done for decades. Once that transformation happens, it is not uncommon for a fourth-quartile bank to achieve top-quartile performance within a few short years—and stay there.

Unfortunately, accountability for the right things rarely happens simply by "hiring good people" and letting them "do their thing."

Most banks try to fix this problem with training. Despite my having won an award for best training program from the Association for Talent Development, "training" is not the answer. Training teaches people what to do—education teaches them how to ***be***. This concept of *being* transcends emotions and limiting beliefs and instead assumes the best from people.

But many banks continue to place their hope in sales training companies or hire a hotshot to "transform the team." Within a year, the sales training company fails, and the hotshot gets fired, despite great talent and attributes. Why? They were set up to fail in a faulty system. Through no doing of their own, they were dropped into a dysfunctional, unsupportive system.

## IT'S ALL A CONFIDENCE GAME

According to Socrates, "human excellence is a state of mind." Performance problems often stem from a lack of confidence. If people don't believe they are worthy to succeed, they *will* self-sabotage.

Many psychologists insist that everyone is a self-saboteur to some degree. The pattern is archetypal, an undeniable pattern within our DNA.

**Therapist Sheri Jacobson explains it well: "Like most forms**

**of defeating thoughts and behaviors, sabotage is largely a pattern from childhood.** It's connected to your 'inner critic'—the voice that tells you that you can't do things or that you aren't good enough. Confidence, or its lack, is connected to core beliefs: the truths you hold about life. Most disturbingly, many people unconsciously make all of life's decisions based on their faulty 'truths.' "

A comedian in a New York comedy club recently said it well: "Every time you hit your finger with a hammer and yell, 'you dumb idiot,' that's your daddy talking." Every man in the audience roared. The comedian called it "daddy issues." They understood that "beliefs" developed in childhood don't always serve them well. If your daddy didn't create a belief system in you that when you do dumb things you are dumb, then likely a teacher, coach, bus driver, or somebody else filled the role. Subsequently, your inner critic created a "belief system" that you're not good enough to achieve results beyond a certain level.

What are the tell-tale signs that you have underperforming team members who hold back in doing what they know to do?

- They *pretend* they don't know what matters. "Oh, was I supposed to bring in the deposits along with that loan?"
- They do the spin cycle all day, every day, never making time for the critical few things that really matter. Their answer to the question "why didn't you complete these important things?" is always "I was busy." *Busy* is a four-letter word.
- They engage in small talk and corporate minutiae, then complain to their families, coworkers, and boss that there's "just too much to do." Do you have a chatterbox who interrupts people all day long? They not only sabotage their own results but also those of everyone within earshot who can't concentrate.
- Lastly, they justify it all with excuses like, "well, the boss has unrealistic expectations" or the ever-popular "nobody told me nuttin'!"

The extreme version of self-sabotaging is the stir-the-pot, gossipy whispers of "I-shouldn't-tell-you-this-but…" conversations. That's the ultimate demonstration that an employee needs to justify underperformance by hurting others—usually by making negative comments about the leaders. Their defaming words and crazy-making activities quickly leave a trail of carnage in your culture whereby people "blame" instead of owning responsibility for what went wrong and learning from it.

If truth be told, occasionally executives are at the core of the self-sabotaging behaviors. They repeat the things that haven't worked for them or for others, hoping for a different result. Their people can't help but be limited by the limited worldview of their leaders.

Over the years, I've heard several bank CEOs proclaim in front of their teams that they can't command premium pricing because the competition is just too tough—they *have to* match rates. With that as the core of their belief system, there's absolutely no way their people will command premium pricing. People will never perform beyond their executives' limited worldview. We've all heard of the elephant trained to stay in an area simply by putting a cuff with a chain around its leg. When the chain is removed, the elephant still stands in place—not even moving to escape a nearby fire.

If you recognize yourself as someone who self-sabotages, welcome to planet Earth. Start by forgiving yourself. Almost every leader has held back their team at some time by being "stuck" in a belief system or a pattern of busy work. It's part of the human condition. Guilt and shame just give you permission to repeat the pattern and subsequently fail again. And if you repeat those limiting belief patterns, there's little to no chance your bank will exist in five to ten years.

Challenging times require that everyone gets infinitely better at everything they do.

As a leader, when it comes to helping your people rise to the next level, you tend to have one of three experiences:

- You *preach* accountability to your team, but you fear being mocked as the village idiot because no one takes accountability for lack of performance. They continue to match rates, fail to earn the entire relationship, and don't make their calls or follow the sales system with extreme attention to detail.
- Or you've made some good progress—people want to perform—but it seems that they really don't know how their work affects the bank's profit. As a result, they're not optimizing their results.
- Or perhaps your bank is doing well; your people are quite good. But good IS the enemy of great. Deep down, you know that you haven't yet tapped into what is possible and what would take you to "superstar" performance and *keep* you there.

Regardless of where you are currently, read on, because soon you'll discover how to create an effective accountability culture, define each employee's critical drivers, and dramatically increase your profit per team member.

## THE CASE FOR ACCOUNTABILITY

As your people start to hold themselves accountable, you'll begin to hear comments like this from a team member in a client organization: "When we first started doing the No More Order Taking™" Sales System, I thought, 'I can't do that.' But now that we've been doing this for a while, I feel like I'm good at it. And I feel *so* good about myself. I feel like I'm making a difference in peoples' lives every single day!"

When people perform at a level beyond what they thought to be their limitations, it builds their self-confidence. This CEO said it best: "Since we started three months ago, our mystery shopping scores went from 3.6 to 9.4. Our cross sales went from 2.2 to 3.8. And our deposits have grown 6 times faster than last year at this time. Our profits are up 19 percent quarter over quarter. But the biggest change of all is that my people feel confident. Now, they think they can do *anything*!"

So how can you begin to build, strengthen, and sustain your accountability culture along with the confidence and joy from purposeful work?

## START WITH CONFIDENCE

So many well-intentioned attempts employ the typical approach to improving accountability. The executive sets clear goals for "officer calls" and results, combined with "training" and better incentive pay. Sound familiar? That "strategy," used by more than a thousand bank CEOs, has an infinitesimal positive impact according to the CEOs themselves! In fact, the approach often has a dramatically negative impact. That is, these approaches create the opposite result of what was intended.

Without a grounding in the roots of industrial psychology and organizational development and without creating a stage-appropriate accountability program, you're unlikely to create the results you want. And if you do see a blip on the accountability radar, know that without a grounded, holistic "franchise system," your bank is vulnerable to the next recession, employee exit, or other bad news.

When we do the orientation call for the Accredited Banking Professional™ certification course, to make it safe for attendees to tell the truth, I start with a confession.

"Listen, I didn't grow up with a silver spoon in my mouth. On the contrary. I grew up on a dairy farm during a deep recession. All our neighbors were losing their farms, and we were barely hanging on. We worked like dogs and never had money. So, when I graduated from college and started as a lender, calling on successful millionaires just a week after graduation, the little voice in my head screamed, “Who the heck do you think you are? You aren’t a millionaire. You don’t know how to help them. They’ll know you’re a fraud.” I felt completely unworthy to add value to the lives of these clients and prospects. I told myself that I hadn’t earned the right to be in front of affluent people.

After my confession, I then ask the class members to raise their hands if they can relate to feeling inadequate to be in front of sophisticated clients and prospects. Without hesitancy, every hand goes up every…single…year. Fascinating! Although some in the course are only a few years into their careers, many of those in the certification program are executives who have been lenders or deposit specialists for decades.

So, time in position is not the answer to confidence and accountability. Neither is having been a commercial lender.

Without the confidence to know that you’re indispensable in your prospects’ lives, you will have only two results: first, self-sabotage by sorting paperclips by color rather than making the calls, or second, self-sabotage by making a minimal number of calls that sound like some version of this: “You wouldn’t want to do business with us, would you? I’m sure you love your current bank. But if you change your mind, call me. Here’s my card.”

The first outcome is common. The second will only serve to support the belief system that you can only get the business if you give it away at a “competitive” (a.k.a. pathetically unprofitable) rate—and only when the incumbent bank fouls up. Not a good strategy.

In the next chapter, you’ll discover how to transform the confidence of your team so that they truly believe they’re worthy of getting the best customers at premium pricing.

CHAPTER ELEVEN

# BUILDING CONFIDENCE FOR AN ACCOUNTABILITY CULTURE

*"I'm no longer accepting the things I cannot change. I am changing the things I cannot accept."*

ANGELA DAVIS

"I don't know what's wrong. I keep telling my people, and telling my people, and telling my people what to do to hit their goals. But no matter how many times I tell them, they aren't improving." This was a recent sad confession from an SVP retail officer.

It is not an uncommon frustration from bright, committed executives doing everything they know to do to help their people and teams hit their goals. When nothing happens, they feel defeated.

In fact, most organizations are strung together with a series of "this too shall pass" initiatives. Whether an attempt to improve the sales culture or to implement new software, oftentimes executives realize only a small fraction of the hoped-for potential.

After executives "tell" their people what to do, a few behaviors change for a short period of time. But many team members don't even participate. The vast majority make a few of the required changes, but only for a brief period. Then become even *less* disciplined about their work habits than before. Eventually senior management gives up, waits a few years, and then rolls out another attempt at the same thing. Only to fail again.

As we start client engagements, many bank CEOs secretly confess that they've made three or more "false attempts" at creating a sales culture. As a result, they feel as though they lose credibility when they even use the word "sales" (as if the word itself is the problem).

Of course, ditching the word "sales" cannot correct the problem. What if the bank had made dozens of accounting errors over the last few decades? Would you decide to stop using the word "accounting"? Hardly—that would be nonsensical.

So, what goes wrong in these ratchet-up-the-sales scenarios that make people simply shrug when the next attempt rolls around? Two things: speed and sustainability.

Most banks lack the know-how to create a significant breakthrough quickly. With an immediate spike in sales, people feel the joy of seeing needles move and experience the satisfaction of accomplishment. But unfortunately, the second obstacle surfaces: The bank lacks the organizational development and franchise systems to keep the momentum going.

## KEEPING THE PLATES IN THE AIR

As you think about these two challenges that banks face in revving up their sales cultures, let me circle back to an era several decades ago. On Sunday evenings, Americans (including my family) sat glued to their televisions to watch Ed Sullivan's "variety" show. We had a black-and-white TV, which incidentally received a signal out in the country from only one channel and only on a clear day.

Even as a toddler at the time, I witnessed two fascinating acts on the TV show: The Beatles debut and a guy with spinning plates. But here was the mind-boggling thing about the plates: The performer tossed the first plate up in the air and grabbed it with a long stick as the plate started downward. He then began to spin that plate atop his stick. Then he tossed up a second plate, caught it with another stick and began to rotate it. Then another. And another. And eventually, when the first plate started to fall, he'd run back to the first stick and tighten up the rotation until it was spinning perfectly again. Before the act ended, he had over a dozen plates spinning on sticks.

Although I don't get as excited about spinning plates now, I do have a new fascination with this phenomenon because it illustrates perfectly the problem that's at the core of sustainable company transformation: The need to make something work flawlessly and quickly and then to develop a system to keep everything going well at once.

So where do you start this transformation in your bank? With something you can improve and perfect quickly. Something extremely visible that affects the customer and builds employee confidence.

## ARREST DECAY AND RESTORE VIGOR ONE FRANCHISE SYSTEM AT A TIME

As Horace put it: "Great effort is required to arrest decay and restore vigor." So, we must "arrest decay" and "restore vigor" one key franchise system at a time.

The idea bears repeating: Do NOT start to transform a system to ensure accountability unless you KNOW you'll move the needle substantially and quickly.

For example, within 24 hours after our proprietary Kick-Butt Kick-Off® event, everyone is very visibly involved in an accountability process whereby the bank will dramatically increase its mystery shopping scores. In fact, in almost 30 years of doing these, every bank but two nearly tripled its scores within three weeks. The other two banks already had scores higher than four, so tripling was impossible, but both of those banks more than doubled their scores.

Immediately upon that breakthrough, customers start to tell your people that they can see the difference. Team members are celebrated, systems are in place for continual improvement, and managers know exactly how to make sure their teams increase their scores. Those managers understand that "managing" doesn't mean only being available to answer questions and do yearly performance reviews. Instead, they know that their effectiveness is rated by how well their teams perform. As a result, they become servant leaders. They serve their people, making sure everyone gets the coaching, education, and encouragement to win.

Once managers and their teams are winning on that first system (Phone Customer Delight Mastery Roll-Out), it's time to start spinning and winning each of the hundred or so other franchise systems.

The bigger game: building confidence, credibility, and accountability, as the "this too shall pass" mantra changes to "This NEW shall not pass!"

Keep reading. The next chapter will give you a process on how to not just make people accountable, but accountable for what matters most—profit *and* purpose.

CHAPTER TWELVE

# MAKING EVERY TEAM MEMBER ACCOUNTABLE FOR PROFIT AND PURPOSE

*"I've never seen a separation between work and play. It's all living."*
RICHARD BRANSON

Have you ever met anyone who didn't want to be healthy, rich, and loved? Enriching relationships are hard to come by. Equally hard to come by are people who understand that when an "effect" (wealth, health, love) doesn't meet expectations, the "cause" is also suspect.

When we don't get the "effect" or "result" we want, it's often because we're blaming circumstances such as the competition, the economy, or the east wind. Translated to banking, the blame game sits at the core of performance below potential.

The key to success is to consistently execute on the right things in the right way at the right time.

## TOP 10 PERCENT ILLUSION

*Businessweek* asked 6,000 employees nationwide the same question: "Do you perform in the top 10 percent in your company?" Of the employees surveyed, between 84 and 97 percent (depending on position) said: "Yes—I'm in the top 10 percent of performers in my company!"

Breaking news: When 84 to 97 percent of your employees believe they perform in the top 10 percent, then "Houston, we have a problem." That problem is that people don't really know how they tie to profit on a daily, weekly, monthly, and quarterly basis. And the *bigger* problem is that they *think* they do.

Prior to my speech at an all-company event, the bank's CEO was addressing his team to "inspire" them to greatness: "... And next year we want an ROA of 1.8." As he said those words, asking for an "effect," it was clear that his team had absolutely no idea how they could be "at cause" to make that effect happen.

## LEADING INDICATORS VERSUS LAGGING INDICATORS

Don Herold's observation comes to mind at this juncture: "Unhappiness is not knowing what we want and killing ourselves to get it." Those team members of the CEO mentioned above will knock themselves out to make things happen—while they and their boss grow steadily unhappier!

It doesn't have to be that way.

Within a year or two, almost every person can, at a minimum, DOUBLE their productivity and the ROI from their payroll dollars. Many can go far beyond that. I've witnessed many increase their performance by as much as five times within a few years. What's more, before transforming their accountability cultures, they would have thought that kind of success impossible.

The key is to focus at the "cause" level, not only on the "effect."

Measuring the right critical drivers is essential but insufficient. You also need a blended educational program tied to a good organizational development system. That means every team member builds skill and confidence one stage at a time. This combination—and ONLY this combination—creates sustained transformation that takes your bank to top performance in every important KPI.

Almost every bank is filled with good, well-meaning people who essentially do their jobs based on what they observed from the previous person in the role. I did it. First, as the only female lender in a sea of men who all did the same thing, I wanted to fit in, so I also jumped in the car, called on owners, and asked them unskilled questions that always led me right to the rate conversation. At that point, there was no way to get the business unless we matched rates. I did exactly what the other lenders did who had been there longer, assuming that they must know how to do their job in the best possible way.

Later, because I was doing "a good job" as a lender, the CEO added to my responsibilities: head of marketing. Now, mind you, even though I'd never had a marketing course, it fell to me to market our entire organization. So, again I did exactly what the guy before me had done. Sadly, I created a negative ROI from the marketing dollars, just as he had.

I meant well. I certainly didn't intend to create a negative ROI. In fact, I didn't even know that was happening. I simply did what I saw every other bank marketer do. Because I hadn't yet read more than a hundred books on marketing to figure out a better approach, I unknowingly wasted the resources of our organization with no nefarious intent.

As an executive, I did exactly what the other executives did. I ran around answering questions from the team instead of proactively leading and aligning people effectively to execute what was most important.

Although I performed at the top of the pack in each of those positions, that assessment wasn't saying much. I simply had no idea about other ways to perform. I just repeated what I saw others before me do.

It's highly likely you and your team members are in that cycle too.

To break that cycle, when setting a goal, don't focus only on the outcome. Instead, focus on what needs to change to accomplish that outcome—the small wins that will make the big win happen faster. Select the right stage-appropriate critical drivers in the right order that are the precursors to the KPIs you desire to impact.

When you collapse the outcomes with what needs to change (effects), you keep harping on the need to change, but it doesn't happen. As a leader, you begin to sound like the CEO who bared his soul to me on his number one priority for almost a decade that remained elusive: "We've been trying to improve our NIM for *nine* years. Every year it's the number one objective on our strategic plan. But every year it remains a struggle."

## WHAT'S THE ACCOUNTABILITY PROBLEM?

First, as I said earlier, new employees tend to get trained by the person who held the job previously, who may not have been a top 5 percent performer. As a result, your high-potential person is not realizing high performance because their education was not *geared* for optimal performance.

Second, your team likely doesn't understand that your top 100 customers account for 50 to 140 percent of your profits (based on stats from research into banks of up to $2 billion in assets). As a result, team members have no plan for how to best spend their time and efforts to get and keep more of those top 100 customers.

## BUSY IS A FOUR-LETTER WORD

Let's face it: When 87 percent of most banks' customers are unprofitable, all the "busy work" activities to bring them in and service them amount to noise. To repeat: "busy" is a four-letter word! We don't want busy—we want productive. It doesn't mean you can't service those customers. It simply means you can't miss on the strategies that bring in your top 100 next-best customers because it gives you the privilege of helping the others.

Third, your operations people probably don't know how their roles tie to profits. Most executives mention that they have no idea how to hold their operations team accountable to profit. As an executive, it's your mission to help your team learn the truth: Every team member has a *revenue* job. They often have the most access to know where your customers and prospects have funds, so that you can seize opportunities. Also, the quantity and quality of the work as well as the service impact of both internal and external customer experiences must be exemplary for an operations person to perform in a way that creates a positive ROI from their salary dollars.

Almost every bank seems to have either no accountability system or accountability that is to the wrong metrics or ones that are not stage-appropriate. If you have that issue, you're not alone, but there are some things you can do to transform your profitability within weeks. Read on.

## THREE STEPS TO HIGH PERFORMANCE AND HIGHER PROFITS

The following three steps will help you gain traction over the next few weeks on aligning each of your teammates to profit.

### Step 1: Double or Triple Your Cross-Sales on New Accounts to Transform Your Efficiency Ratio

This is an example of a critical driver moving a KPI: a "cause" that leads to an "effect."

Despite what you may have heard as conventional wisdom, the best way to improve your efficiency ratio is *not* tightening salaries, laying off people, or cutting expenses for marketing, travel, and training. In fact, those cuts are what pushed many banks to extinction during the last recession. Challenging times require "leaning in" as opposed to retracting. You can only cut expenses so much—the answer to difficult economic times is always predictable, profitable, and safe revenue.

If cutting any cost hurts your productivity and culture long-term, don't even consider that course of action. Sadly, the end of a recession is when those banks meet their maker. They may have hung on longer, but they will lose their independence regardless because you can't cost-cut your way through a deeply challenging time.

Usually about one year into working with a bank, as we review their numbers during a strategic advancement call, it gives me great joy to see the executives discover that they shaved 10 basis points off their efficiency ratio. Typically, it's a surprise to them because they may not have been consciously attempting an improved efficiency ratio. They thought the only way to improve the efficiency ratio was to cut costs. In fact, they are often thrilled to discover that the best way to achieve a lower efficiency ratio is to increase profitable revenue. They often don't teach that in Graduate Schools of Banking, but they should!

### Step 2: Identify the Top 10 Percent of Activities for Every Job in Your Institution

These priority activities will bring in the low-hanging fruit. Don't think that the next gadget, software program, or tool will lead to more profit per employee: The reality is that most people are rather distracted by items that are clearly not the highest and best use of their time.

Here's a familiar example of wasted time in most banks. Lenders sit behind their desks or only respond to the calls that come in. Usually those credits are B and C quality: A+ loans rarely come looking for you.

Your lenders task your credit analysts with preparing to take a loan to the loan committee. Long hours are spent on a loan that, if closed, will bring risk to the institution—a real cost to your bank. Then, it goes to committee and you need to get "creative" to find out how to make it while protecting you from the higher risk. Then, IF the loan gets approved—and many won't, so imagine all the lost time and expense for those— the lender then goes back to say the deal was approved, and then the negotiating begins. And they now want you to do it at an even better price.

It is no wonder that those lenders create a negative ROI from their salary dollars compared to those who are proficient at closing top 100 or top 1000 prospects at premium pricing—assuring both safety and profitability with no wasted time.

We've seen banks double in size within three to five years, while keeping the same headcount simply by figuring out how to create stage-appropriate accountability and by developing people so that they can perform with a level of mastery. As important, if not more so, is the fact that people will go home every night feeling like superstars: Souls will be fed.

### Step 3: Start the Transformation Process with the Fastest Path to the Money—The Jobs Producing the Highest Revenue

Give those people the necessary skills and make sure to clarify what success looks like in their positions.

While your entire team would likely benefit from far more awareness of how they tie to profit and, more importantly, how to do their work in a way that actually achieves the best results, the place to start is those people on your team that have the biggest impact on improving revenue and the profitability of that revenue. That can be an immediate game changer.

For example, if a commercial banker can increase new business added annually from $15 million to $35 million—and get 100+

basis points more on exceptional *quality* loans—that's a massive move impacting profitability. Clearly, that has a bigger impact than improving the quality and quantity of output in a low-level operations position. Sustainable profitability, however, requires accountability to be driven throughout the entire organization eventually.

It is the job of the bank executive team to figure out how to create results regardless of circumstances. That's why executives exist.

Results come from focus, and they require mastery of skillsets and overcoming limiting beliefs while focusing on the right things done right.

Results trump activity. Results trump excuses. Results RULE.

In the next chapter, we will tackle how to achieve profitable organic loan growth—one of the most important areas to master to drive accountability to profit.

CHAPTER THIRTEEN

# DEBUNKING THE FIVE BIGGEST MYTHS IN LOAN GROWTH

*"If we want to reach people no one else is reaching, we've got to do things no one else is doing."*

ANDY STANLEY

"We can do this deal as long as we match the rates." By the time someone makes this statement, it's usually true.

But what if there was a way that your team could keep from being backed into that corner? What if there was a system that almost guarantees that you don't have to match rates ever again… even on your very *best* credits?

At this point, most lenders feel tempted to stop reading. They *know* it can't be done, and they have a mountain of "evidence" to prove it.

In contrast, most board members and CEOs lean in here. They worry about Hovde's comment about the trend line of the diminishing number of community banks: "If we continue the current trend, we'll be down to one bank in 25 years." Executives know that they must figure out this "rate matching" conundrum before their bank loses its franchise and gets swept into another bank.

As someone who started her career as a commercial and

agricultural lender, I can assure you that there are some common myths that I believed and that commercial bankers and chief lending officers still believe today:

**Myth 1:** You must match the rate to get the deal.

**Myth 2:** If customers like their current bank, you'll need to wait for the incumbent to make an error before you have a chance for their business.

**Myth 3:** It's a numbers game.

**Myth 4:** Sales training will help solve the problem.

**Myth 5:** Incentive pay is the answer to motivating performers.

Stay with me here as I debunk each of these myths. There is a new emerging mountain of evidence highlighting banks that are pulling ahead of competitors who still believe these myths.

### Myth 1: You must match the rate to get the deal.

This is true… until it is not. Matching rates is necessary for bankers who don't know how to get out of the commodity pricing trap.

The secret to getting out of "rate-matching hell" is in how you manage the first meeting—in fact, the first few words you utter in that first meeting. The right approach in that first customer exchange will elevate your standing so that you get the respect you deserve.

The answer is not slapping the prospect's back while you mouth those standard, pathetic, and never-believed lines: "We have good people" and "We have good customer service." At this point, the customer has no "social proof" those statements are true. And even if those clichés were accepted as true, at best, that might get you an extra 25 basis points on a loan and an even smaller impact on deposits.

To keep your franchise thriving, your team needs to figure out how to get a full 150 extra basis points or more on A+ quality credits. It is the banks that figure this out that will protect their independence over the next few decades.

More than a dozen banks have told me about their failed attempts to fix this rate-matching problem, some bringing in as many as three or more different sales training companies. In a few cases, the training company had to be dismissed immediately because of the damage it was doing, even though the bank was obligated to continue paying them.

With gimmicky approaches such as "feel, felt, found" formulas, a "feature versus benefit" explanation, or the "what keeps you up at night?" questioning routine, traditional training accomplishes two things:

1. It makes the customer or prospect feel violated in the relationship because they know they're being worked.
2. Equally bad, if not worse, it makes your team feels violated because they've been reduced to the demeaning approach of used car salespeople.

Such tactics replace the soul-to-soul communication that allows the customer relationship to grow. Customers need to have a deep, gut-level sense that you thoroughly understand their concerns and are sharing wisdom while making indispensable recommendations—not just pushing the "product of the month." If your people aren't bringing in six cross-sales on each new account, you can be assured they are not being perceived as a source of indispensable wisdom.

Don't even consider sales training without a holistic system that includes integration of these truly transformative strategies:

- High-ROI marketing that can reduce the marketing budget by as much as 80 percent while dramatically increasing sales to profitable new customers
- Organizational development principles to create an ever-increasing culture score
- Stage-appropriate accountability
- Confidence-building systems to require high levels of outcomes every quarter
- A tie-everyone-to-profit blended learning system tied to stage-appropriate accountability

Of course, if your bank doesn't have dozens of unique selling propositions (USPs) to differentiate, and it lacks a sales process proven to command premium pricing on prospects who love their current banks, then you won't be able to get the additional 150 basis points on the loan along with the low-cost deposits.

Lastly, the only way to get premium pricing at a close rate north of 85 percent on A+ quality credits is meticulous execution of the sales process geared to command that pricing and close rate. Most banks have entirely too much "slop" in their system, and even more have the wrong system or none at all.

Sales IS a system, and winning big deals at premium pricing requires flawless execution of that system. Imagine closing the books at the end of the quarter by telling your team: "Hey, just you do whatever you want to close the books and let's see how it goes." Painful thought, right? The sales process requires the same meticulous execution that your accounting team uses to close the books.

**Myth 2: If customers like their current bank, you'll need to wait for the incumbent to make an error before you have a chance at the business.**

Since 87 percent of bank customers lose money for the bank,

it should seem fairly clear that the only game in town is pulling your competitors' best customers away from them with no chance of them coming back to "rescue the deal" and undercutting your pricing after you have a deal. In fact, you'd better master this really fast if you want to keep your banking franchise independent. Frankly, the only prospects you really *want* are those who *are* happy with their current banks—banks typically take good care of their best customers.

If your people believe that they have to wait for a mistake, the conversation goes something like this: "Okay, so it sounds like you're fairly happy with your current bank. Here's my card. Please call me if that ever changes." Heartbreaking, isn't it? These lenders demean themselves as unworthy of the first-place ribbon. Thousands of bankers follow this exact script every…single…day.

The error repeated by most banks is that they send in a minimally prepared person or team to call on an affluent prospect. Very aware of the value of time, affluent people won't tolerate anyone wasting it. They have little patience for lenders who don't get to the point about how changing banks immediately can add significant value to their business. If it is not clear to the prospect that it's a no-brainer to switch, they will politely end the conversation with: "I'll think it over."

If your person or team calls on a "top 100 prospect," you can be assured that if they don't close that deal by the second appointment, they likely won't get invited back to the table for the next decade. Your bank will be "branded" as a waste of time.

As a sales manager, your key performance indicators should include the following:

- Appointment set rate on top 100 prospects
- Second meeting on top 100 prospects
- Close rate at premium pricing within two weeks of the second appointment
- Total dollars of weighted sales funnel on top 100 prospects

- Total dollars closed on top 100 prospects YTD
- Cross-sales on new top 100 prospects closed

Quite frankly, those are the most important leading indicators in your business. Most banks find that they don't even know how to identify their top 100 next best customers, and they certainly aren't making enough traction at closing at least 30 percent of them every year with an 85 per close rate.

Banks talk about their lagging indicators of loan growth, deposit growth, NIM, ROA, ROE, and efficiency ratio. The reality is that without mastery of the above leading indicators, their only success depends on their competitor's mistakes or positive economic impact—they are not managing the resources of the institution to create a "predictable success machine." Instead, they pat themselves on the back during good times or when competitors do silly things and blame the economy when things are bad.

### Myth 3: It's a numbers game

For three decades now, I've been speaking at bank CEO conferences. The one thing I can count on at each conference is hearing someone utter these words: "officer call program." Heads nod. Pens smoke as attendees jot this idea in their notebooks. Then the same people return to the conference the following year to repeat the same scenario.

At some point, this scene begs the question: If it's such a good idea, why isn't it working?

Granted, on some level, officer calls are necessary. But most of them are merely "howdy doody" calls, whereby the only outcome is that the doughnuts your people bring make prospects pre-diabetic. No other outcome is measurable.

Then the lender stalks into the sales meeting proudly announcing he's made an "officer call" and the prospect is "thinking about it." That prospect then stays in the funnel for months, sometimes years…while they enjoy free golf, doughnuts, and lunches, each time assuring the lender they'll continue to "think about it."

Selling is not a numbers game—it is a game of sophistication, whereby the lender moves from being a transactional banker to a transformational banker and works a predictable process that assures that they will close with a predictable close rate. In this game, after the banker leaves the initial meeting, the prospect is deeply disturbed about the gap between your Level 4 USP and what their current bank is providing. That prospect feels deprived and upset about the substantial costs of not having what your bank offers.

For a moment, consider what goes wrong with "officer call programs."

**Lenders call on the wrong people.** Yes, it's nice to feel welcome when calling on the same people month after month and year after year. Many of those prospects are just too polite to say "no," so they kindly welcome the lender into their businesses for a second chat—or even a seventh one.

Alternatively, lenders adopt the misguided "let's call on everybody up and down the street" approach. But rarely are the most desirable prospects found on the same street. Rather than geographic location, the best prospects tend to share the same psychographics and firmographics, which must be carefully identified.

**Lenders fail to build reputational equity.** At best, cold-calling positions your lenders as "vendors." If you're calling on someone who isn't yet terribly excited to meet with you, it's likely because you've not put the "Top 100 Reputational Equity Strategy" in place. Instead, you've put yourself in a difficult position to escape. Even though you may close a few loans, not many will close at and your close rate will most definitely be far below 85 to 90 percent. You've positioned yourself as a vendor before the party even started.

**Lenders provide you with details about the prospect to justify why they're still in the sales funnel.** The purpose of the sales meeting is to tighten disciplines and ensure that every step is executed with precision. The only comments in sales meetings should be like these: "I'm now at the point where the prospect has told us that X element of USP 4 is worth $750,000 to them and that Y element is worth $450,000."

If, instead, your lenders are saying things like the following, they're in trouble: "And Eddie's uncle used to go fishing with my Uncle Louie. I also saw his plant, and he has a real nice operation there." That kind of extraneous information suggests that the lending officer is not adhering to the sales process. Sales meetings are about sharing the exactness to the sales process so that any deviations can be sorted out before the deal is lost or dragged into "rate-matching hell."

Yes, most banks need a few more calls to create better results. However, almost every bank would be far better served by dramatically improving the *quality* of their calls.

### Myth 4: Sales training will help

When loan growth is not optimal, sometimes the "strategy" is to hire more lenders. That too often means that you pay a huge recruiting fee, along with a signing bonus, to bring in a "superstar" with a portfolio. A year later, very little of that promised portfolio has moved over to your bank, and the only loans that person made are endangering the quality of the portfolio. Ninety percent of the time, that "superstar" lender is terminated after a year. (Incidentally, when I mention that in speeches, almost every head in the room nods. After the speech, several come up and secretly confess that they thought it was only they who continued to make this misguided move.)

So, if hiring more people is not the answer, executives move to another "logical" step: "Let's try sales training." The result? Almost without exception, when executives hire a sales training firm, the bank reports minimal to no change. If there is an improvement, it is short-lived.

Of course, sales training *should* work. Experts carrying their "I'm a sales trainer" cards cold call the bank—a sure sign that their program doesn't work—and then present their proposal to "rope the moon," fixing your sales issues for good. What they often forget to mention is that they don't own a rope.

The "sales tricks" they tout demonstrate that they don't understand banking, which is far more complex than their tricks can address. To be specific, here are some questions the sales trainers don't answer well:

- How are you at identifying your next best prospects?
- How will you create mental readiness for the entire team—not just the sales team? If you work for a bank, you're on the sales team. Imagine that you have a lender working on a $7 million deal, and that the prospect calls the bank only to be met by a friendly staffer who has no idea how to convert this conversation to one of value. Deal lost. Nobody really knows why. It happens every single day.
- How will you handle the "I've got this" folks? Every bank has a few of those "been around a long time and I've seen things come and go, so you just do what I'm doing" folks. They take over the break room. They get at the "youngins" usually within days, before their high spirits start to create results that exceed those of the "old-timers."

Often, if you really analyze those old-timers' portfolios, you'll discover that they aren't bringing in a lot of new business from new sources. And most of their portfolios, with few A+ quality credits, were won by price-matching. In fact, many of them have terrible close rates and atrocious results in commanding premium pricing—they're just sitting on a fat portfolio, much of which was handed to them.

Those with the old-timer attitude fear discovery, but they're smart enough to realize that their best move is to disenfranchise the newbies before they become hotshots. They are often *very* skilled at doing exactly that—they've mastered passive-aggressive ways.

If you have old-timers preying on the psyche of newcomers, sales training isn't going to stop it. Hiring another sales training firm will only aggravate the problem.

If some executive with a short memory pipes up yet again with "sales training is the answer," there goes the next pot-load of money and time flushed down the toilet, as your competitors pull even further ahead. You approach must be proven to "enroll" the entire team to using one sales process—the one that works.

"Results follow money." That gets said at least a thousand times a year at bank conferences. Yet when I ask bank CEOs if incentive pay fixed their low growth problems, the answer is a resounding "no."

Illogical? Maybe. The truth? Yes. Of course, incentive pay *can* make a small dent for a short period of time. However, most every incentive program out there that inspires green creates the opposite effect: self-absorbed, self-centered mavericks, who think of the bank's customers as "their" customers and who protect "their" portfolio at the risk of damaging the bank's performance, profitability, and safety.

The problem is that these programs miss a key principle I studied during graduate work in organizational development: Extrinsic awards (like cash and prizes) *only* work if somebody isn't paid enough. Intrinsic rewards (feeling good about doing the right thing) have a sustainable and powerful long-term impact.

I'm not saying that incentive pay should be verboten in all banks. What I am saying is that such programs—especially those that have the primary focus only on individual pay—are not the total answer or even the best one. Typically, the best incentive programs tie individual metrics to team contributions and the bank's overall performance. Individuals don't win unless the team wins.

That said, before structuring an incentive program, look first to your emotional intelligence scores and the associated Human Capital Audit. Make sure that you adjust your incentive program to align with the uniqueness of your sales members and teams. Those with low self-awareness scores will be most motivated by team performance and team incentives. Those with high self-awareness scores will be more motivated by individual performance incentives and recognition. That's why a combination of individuals with team incentives works best.

After decades of working with us, many high-performing banks with some of the highest-performing lenders report that they still offer *no* incentive pay program. When I asked a CEO recently what their incentive pay program was, the response was: "When we took it out, results went up."

Complex problems cannot be handled with pedestrian solutions. When banks try to solve a revenue problem with simplistic answers, I can predict with great accuracy that they'll continue to have those problem for years. Only through holistic approaches of organization development, Smarketing, and the right sales system executed with precision will banks create a permanent path to revenue growth.

We've recorded a five-part loan-growth video course designed for you to watch with your executive team. It will help you get everyone focused on the right next actions to spur loan growth—both profitably and safely. Get instant access to the video series at: **https://EmmerichFinancial.com/bbtoolkit**

CHAPTER FOURTEEN

# TEAM SELLING TRUMPS INDIVIDUAL SELLING MODEL

*"Not finance. Not strategy. Not technology. It is teamwork that remains the ultimate competitive advantage—both because it is so powerful and so rare."*

PATRICK LENCIONI

What if your sales strategy is antiquated and functioning at a small fraction of its potential as a result?

Research in other industries is clear regarding complex sales such as commercial relationships: Team selling crushes the individual selling model in terms of both revenue and profit. A *Harvard Business Review* article entitled "Why Individuals No Longer Rule on Sales Teams" cited research over 10 years showing that "network" performance now accounts for about 44 percent of the impact on sales.

You'll likely agree that what is repeated as "the unchallenged system" in most banks today not only stymies potential, but also crushes the spirits of your people. It keeps your culture from making your bank a "best place to work."

Most banks find that, if they have a team of 50 commercial lenders, typically somewhere around three of them bring in roughly 70-80% of new business. That's not an anomaly.

While the strategic plans of thousands of banks say they will "grow loans and deposits" by hiring more lenders, most will tell you— if they do the math—that this strategy creates a negative ROI. In the previous scenario, you already have 47 lenders who are not paying for themselves, so the odds aren't good that hiring more lenders will create a positive ROI from the additional salary dollars invested.

Think about it: Most lenders will wander for years "trying" to build a portfolio—never quite offsetting their salary by creating a positive ROI from volume or premium pricing.

Worse yet, if you bring in heavy hitters from competitors who promise their portfolios will come along with them, you have even more risk than with the "wanderers." You'll pay big bucks for that portfolio promise, even though hundreds of CEOs say that the heavy hitters typically don't deliver on their promise to bring that portfolio over. That's true far more often than not.

## MATCHING RATES: THE RACE TO ZERO (PROFIT)

If those heavy hitters do bring some business over, the lender almost always has to match rates to get the deals. That's bad news. Even worse, a lender who can't bring over those deals starts to get itchy after six months. She feels the pressure to pay for her salary. Thinking someone is certainly about to notice, she begins working desperately to bring in *any* low-quality loans, which usually means that the risks of any new business about to be brought on far exceed any pricing she can get.

Let's be clear: The goal of salespeople is to command premium pricing. Why are we paying them if not for their contribution to profit? It's the marketing department that solicits interest from the targeted prospects and builds the reputational equity prior to the first call, but the salesperson is paid to close the deal with premium pricing. Period. That IS the job.

Even if that lender is an exception who does bring over a good chunk of her portfolio, it should not be lost on you that she can leave you in the future and take that portfolio with her. At this point, she's already proven she can do that. History repeats itself.

Then, when a large percentage of lenders aren't closing large, low-risk deals at premium pricing, the next year's strategic plan has an ingenious non-strategy listed: "Hire more lenders." The crazy cycle starts all over again, like that Lamb Chop song: "This is the song that never ends...."

## WHY THE INDIVIDUAL SALES MODEL NO LONGER WORKS

First, we hire everyone into the same title—"Commercial Lender"—and require them to do all the same duties as everyone else with that title, including business development, account management, analysis, deposit gathering, loan workouts, renewals, and "other duties as assigned."

The problem? The emotional intelligence that makes a lender good at business development causes them to be bored and ineffective at account management. An effective business development lender who secures $150 million in new loans in a couple of years becomes "saddled" with renewing her portfolio. She's no longer doing what she loves and does well: The racehorse is now hooked to a plow, circling the field for the rest of her career. Since those with a business development profile are only six percent of the population, according to emotional intelligence assessments, why would a cogent executive have someone who scores low-risk for business development do anything other than business development all day, every day?

Alternatively, there is the account manager, a.k.a., the "farmer" profile. That person loves nurturing relationships and is good at renewing and upselling, but he'll find almost any form of busy work to justify not calling on potential new leads. Even when he does make a few calls, he's not very good at calling on prospects, rarely gets the deals, and when he does, it's hardly ever at premium pricing and with the entire relationship.

With no portfolio to manage (because he hasn't developed one and isn't interested in doing so), he's likely to be put on a "Performance Improvement Plan" to comply with the required number of calls. That's like putting a 5' 6" basketball player on a performance improvement plan, telling him he needs to be 7' 4" within 30 days. There's nothing sane about such placements, yet they happen in banks across this country every single day. And that's only the beginning of what doesn't work.

The next predictable strategic error is requiring those lenders to get more deposits. Every rational executive in a strategic planning session will think "this should be easy—we'll just offer incentives and tell them to bring in deposits with the loans." If Santa and the Tooth Fairy regularly stop by your house, then keep doing that to attract deposits, but remember the research, which says that it typically doesn't work. And if it does work on occasion, those personalities are highly ineffective at fully penetrating the entire relationship. And securing the entire banking relationship upon the first account opening should *always* be the objective.

If you have any of these problems, you're not alone. Almost all the bank executives I've talked to over the course of decades have shared their exasperation regarding the ability to get their commercial teams to magnetically attract quality loans at premium pricing along with low-cost deposits. They all share that they thought they were the only ones not achieving a breakthrough.

So, what's wrong with the traditional approach? Three things.

**First, most lenders lack the humility to tell you that they really don't understand their deposit products.** Despite their need to get that information, they sure won't confess that to the people who are "beneath them" (in their minds). But that's only a small part of the problem.

**Second, they treat other products as ancillary.** The lender thinks of the prospect as "his" customer, so he doesn't even bring up all the other products and how they can solve a small business owner's problems until after the loan is approved or closed. He hesitates despite the fact that the small business owner has specific needs, some unknown and some already identified.

As a result, the lender misses the consultative "I'm on your side, and I'm REALLY good at bringing all the solutions to rock your world" opportunity. Sure, he can strong-arm a prospect: "Our bank requires your deposits to be with us." But what customer enjoys an obligation as opposed to being enthralled with the idea?

**Third, they approach it as a loan transaction.** Because they're bringing in the loan first, without following a sales process that allows the Level 4 USP to justify substantially increased pricing that creates a massive ROI from the extra dollars they pay your bank, these lenders tend to be rate matchers on the loan side. Worse yet, when they do bring up deposits, it sounds like they are "selling.".

To add insult to injury, they're not regularly getting the entire relationship at "hello." That costs you the profitability of the transaction, both in terms of cross-sales and premium pricing.

And all that is just the start regarding why this individual approach doesn't work well.

Other banks say they will fix the problem by having a cash management specialist go on calls with all lenders. While this is technically a team (because it is more than one person), a lender and a cash management specialist are still a weak alternative to an optimized team-selling approach. It's like bringing a rubber band gun to fend off grenades.

When the idea of team selling is brought up, some bank executives say "yup, we do team selling. We send out teams." But their approach is far from what is needed, and it shows up in their close rate at premium pricing.

A team selling process is a complex flow involving many skilled people who know exactly what to do and when to execute on the sales process. Besides, every bank has a cash management person they can parade in front of the prospect, so that's hardly enough differentiation to entice prospects to switch banks while paying a substantial premium.

The bottom line is that the highest-performing banks in the country are systematically using an optimized team-selling approach to achieve over 85 percent close rates and the entire relationship plus 100-150 basis points more than the competition. That closing rate holds even if that prospect starts off saying: "Not interested. I love my current bank." They also gauge to make sure they average at least six cross-sales. Those are the metrics to index against to see if your system is working as it should or whether you have the wrong system.

## TEAM SELLING IS MUCH MORE COMPLEX THAN PUTTING TOGETHER TEAMS

Team selling doesn't mean just putting together a "calling team"—lender and cash management specialist—and hoping for a game-changing result. Although some banks think that's the answer, they miss a key concept: They fail to consider the sophistication and power of team selection based on individual roles and what makes team selling work. Doubling the number of people to do the same work misses this important point entirely.

Regardless of your reason for not doing team selling today—too large, too small, distant locations, don't know how, etc.—it's likely that within the next five years, every top-quartile-performing bank will have ditched the old-school approach and mastered team selling.

If you're ready to implement a team-selling approach, download a complete checklist to get started at: **https://EmmerichFinancial.com/bbtoolkit**

CHAPTER FIFTEEN

# HOW TO DOUBLE CROSS-SALES IN FIVE MONTHS OR LESS

*"Selling is really about having conversations with people and helping improve their company or their life. If you look at it like that, selling is a very admirable thing to do.*

LORI RICHARDSON

When done ethically, good sales results are an indicator of having made a positive impact on the lives of your customers. People inherently feel good when they help others.

A personal banker answered the phone one time when I called for the CEO. She gushed: "Do you mind if I tell you something? At your event, when you taught us how to do the sales process, I thought 'oh gosh, I don't know if I can sell.' But now that we're doing the process, we all feel great about ourselves. We feel like we're helping people."

Helping, indeed.

Quite frankly, most bankers are terrible at selling, which means they're not that good at helping people. That's often because reputable, caring bankers are turned off by *sleazy* sales strategies and techniques, and they don't know that correct sales processes are the most ethical and helpful thing you can do to positively impact customers.

Traditional sales tactics taught by most sales training companies don't belong in community banks—businesses built on trust.

## CROSS-SALES IS THE ULTIMATE MEASURE OF TRUST

Helping a customer so they don't need to go elsewhere to do any of their banking is a noble service. Therefore, cross-sales is the ultimate measure of customer trust.

If your customers recognize that your clear value propositions exceed what your competition offers, then they'll likely trust you and bring all their business to you.

## THE CHALLENGES OF CROSS-SALES

Although bank executives have aspired to get their teams to own the entire relationship for decades, most banks still haven't moved their cross-sales rates beyond 2.2 products per household when they open a new account. If someone is skilled and masterful, a new customer who walks in the door should hit an average cross-sales rate of 5 to 6. At 2.2, those new customers consider your bank to be a "vendor"—not a strategic partner.

Why does this recurring problem not get solved at most banks? Two reasons:

- **Sales-Attempt Fatigue:** Millions of dollars have been spent on "attempts" at improving sales cultures in banks, yet only a few hundred banks have averaged more than 6 cross-sales with each new account opened. The odds of another attempt working, after a history of failures, seem miniscule.
- **A Track Record of Underperformance:** Some banks have been underperforming for so long that they don't believe

> owning the customer relationship is possible—ever! Sadly, the customers are the ones who suffer. They run around town doing business with a handful of "vendor" banks because they believe that no single bank really has their back.

Versions of these same sad stories have popped up 3,000 to 4,000 times as I've talked with bank executives over the last few decades. The situation is prevalent—and totally unnecessary.

## A NON-SALESY APPROACH TO GROWING SALES

Contrary to most sales training that can get you in trouble with prospects—"sales-speak" triggers distrust—you need a much more elegant sales process. Nobody wants to feel manipulated, and especially not by their banker. **If it feels like sales, you are doing it wrong.** If you're selling in a way that people want to buy, they'll never feel like someone is "selling" to them.

*Proper* education solves that typical sales problem of two end results: no sales or slimy sales. Note that I didn't say *training*. Training is, essentially, what to *do*; education, alternatively, is how to *be*. Your team will need to develop their sense of how to *be* with a customer so that the customer feels understood, feels the banker's concern for their situation, and feels strongly that their banker has brought wisdom and direction to the table. The customer must believe that the solutions you offer will, in fact, be of extreme value—far beyond what they received elsewhere.

## THREE STEPS TO DOUBLE CROSS-SALES QUICKLY AND INCREASE THE EXPERIENCE OF TRUST IMMEASURABLY

The following three steps will solve your stagnated cross-sales problem, allowing you to double results in just weeks.

### Step 1: Be a Contrarian

Forget what you believe to be true regarding cross-sales or what folks tell you is true with zero evidence. Many bank CEOs share common approaches when they want more cross-sales. They do the following:

- Hire a sales training company
- Create an incentive program
- Set some goals

If that conventional approach had ever once worked, it might be worth a try. But after talking to thousands of executives and board members, I have yet to hear anyone tell me that the conventional approach has had significant short-term effects, and I've never heard that it had long-term impact. And long-term impact, of course, is the goal!

So, before you sign that contract with a sales trainer, ask them to show you what percentage of their clients have doubled their cross-sales on new accounts within six months. (In God we trust—all others, show me the data!) If they have that proof, then ask to see the long-term sustainability.

If the percentage of the sales training firm's clients that achieved that result is not more than 70-90 percent, know that you're at risk for losing good employees and customers alike. Sales done incorrectly is a disaster culturally and for the client experience. Then, once the inevitable failure happens, you also risk losing your chance to improve your cross-sales…which, of course, you still need to do.

Unlike so many programs that follow traditional "badda bing, badda boom sales training" approaches, you need one that's specialized for the sophistication of high-performing community banking. Your sales program should *never* feel like sales, and it should get the inquirer to stop thinking about rates as the primary selling point.

Most traditional sales training feels like a violation of the humans involved—people hate it. So, it always warms my heart when I get emails from our member banks that say: "We all feel so good about what we're doing now—we feel like we're helping people." That's the way a good sales experience should feel for both parties.

### Step 2: Start Your Sales Transformation with a Cultural Transformation

In many organizations, a new initiative meets some resistance. When you bring sales education to the table as an initiative, you can't afford to have the "Thank you for sharing but I like my way" people who end up being a drag on your performance breakthrough.

A cultural transformation must happen first—one whereby people stop telling you what can't be done and instead chant: "Bring it ON!"

All sales improvement starts with a cultural transformation whereby people make a shift to be more open to being challenged with advanced execution and performance requirements as a part of their jobs. Without an opening, any good education will only create a small shift of performance.

On deeper reflection, how could sales training possibly work without a cultural shift that gets people enthused about growing quickly and being of far more service to their customers?

If you offer training first without a dramatic readiness shift, you will have people hear the need to change as:

- "What you're doing isn't good enough."
- "Your results will be visible now."
- "We'll be expecting much more from you in the very near future."

Is it any wonder that they run for the hills, and most banks lose a third of their team within the first year of a sales training initiative?

### Step 3: Create Predictable Cross-Sales Improvement

After your transformative event whereby your team members rise to a substantially better way of "being" with each other and customers—we call our event the Kick-Butt Kick-Off® event—it is time to have them feel great about "seeing a needle move." This is evidence that they can create substantially improved results.

With one of the largest databases on bank mystery shopping, BankShop® reveals that the average mystery shopping score in America falls somewhere between 3.2 to 3.8 out of 10, depending on the year. The mystery shopping done by BankShop does not just reflect the customer experience but also how effective the person is in helping customers buy by making an impact on that customer's life.

Banks that use traditional mystery shopping that shows them averaging over 8 are typically appalled to see their *real* scores. They soon learn what's required to turn an inquiry into a full relationship. While most banks pound their chests in pride about high scores obtained using low-bar traditional mystery shopping, BankShop scores reflect research on behaviors proven to help convert those asking for a rate to full-relationship customers. And that, of course, is the real reason you invest the money on mystery shopping. Done correctly, it is one of the highest ROI investments a bank can make.

One or two conversions of an inquirer that turns into a $3 million customer can pay for years of shopping. Sadly, for most banks, their mystery shopping is a cost center.

Let's face it: The mystery shopper may like your people and find them delightful. However, if the prospect doesn't bring all their business to you quickly, you're holding a shopping report that doesn't correlate to profit and growth.

When we review the shops from banks that come to our open seminars, they often have already told us authoritatively "we have great people" and "we have great service scores." Yet the scores average in the 3.2-4.0 range.

Before you start any sales initiatives, your mystery shopping scores should average over 9 for every single position in your bank. If you can't get that done in six weeks, do *not* proceed with sales training. With scores lower than 9, the team members have shown you that they have no intention of doing what is expected. You can only imagine how things will go when you ask them to follow new disciplines to take far better care of your prospects and clients that require even more skills.

Not getting this first step correct and then moving on to sales training is similar to telling someone: "Yes, I know you still don't know how to tie your shoes correctly but we're going to have you slap those things on, and tomorrow you will run a marathon."

If you don't start that next step of sales training with a base of mastery of a basic such as how to answer the phone when someone calls and says they want to do business with you, you've taught your people that the upcoming "training" is for their entertainment—not to drive expected behavior changes. The inevitable result: They "slow walk" you on yet another sales training attempt, repeating the mantra "this too shall pass."

This resistance makes no sense until you understand the "why." Quite frankly, people don't want to be held accountable if they think they can't win. And without the right system in place, they can't win. Thus, their desire, whether conscious or unconscious, is to sabotage your efforts to measure performance.

## CONFIDENCE IS THE FOUNDATION

Don't measure performance until you've begun a proven performance intervention whereby you set them up to win. Confidence is the foundation.

If you attempt and fail, the second attempt will be at least two or three times as hard, and the third false attempt will solidify that fact that "they won." Bottom-line: They have enough proof that you'll keep giving up.

However, after the entire system is deployed to make sure that those mystery-shopping scores skyrocket, then your team will be open and ready for effective cross-selling systems. They'll realize that sales really is just the next level of "taking care of people." It's what all good service entails. And when this transformation happens, they'll delight in the intrinsic rewards of knowing that their work is masterful and that they have a powerful impact on each person they touch.

So, build your cross-sales on a firm foundation, as evidenced by strong mystery shopping scores.

When we do our proprietary Kick-Butt Kick-Off® event, we show bank executives the few things they need to do to create a predictable, profound breakthrough within weeks. In 30 years, we haven't had a single bank that hasn't doubled their mystery shopping scores. In fact, roughly 92 percent have tripled those scores!

When *all* team members shoot past a score of 9, your whole community begins to buzz about the "remarkable" service they can't stop talking about. In contrast, without the foundation of having every person master the basics on the phones to help people buy in, sales training will just be an expensive, alienating, lose-good-people-fast train wreck. Plus, you'll have disgruntled employees and upset customers who will feel "sold to." The *last* thing you need at your bank is the "salesy" branding.

## ADDRESS THE ELEPHANT IN THE ROOM

There was a time when a mega-bank received bad press for its cross-sales practices. Likely, someone on your team will bring that situation up and righteously declare that because they are a good person, they won't do cross-sales, thank you very much.

The reality is that anything can be used for good or for evil. Water to drink is good; water that's flooding your basement is bad. Sun feeds the flowers but can burn your skin. Darkness in your bedroom aids your sleep, but darkness in an alley aids a thief.

By the same token, if someone uses cross-sales to line their pockets when they sell things inappropriately, that's a horrendous violation of customer trust. But that doesn't mean cross-selling itself can't help your customers thrive financially.

Let's face it: The average customer has roughly 16 financial products and services. If you have only four, you're not *really* their banker. Let your team know that when it comes to sales, it's not an "either/or" issue but a "both/and" issue. That is, you can help people buy all they need to optimize their financial situation *and* never feel like you're "selling." If you don't have the entire relationship, that means you haven't yet earned their trust. You remain *a vendor*—not *their banker*.

Just because a big bank got bad press regarding cross-sales doesn't mean that you don't have an ethical obligation to help customers buy everything they need to accomplish their goals. And because of that obligation, cross-sales is the ultimate measure of trust.

Start the No More Order Taking 7-Step Sales™ process only after cultural readiness, a huge boost of performance in mystery shopping, and the excitement generated from the profound movement of that needle. Then your team is ready for the necessary education about how to help your prospects and customers buy.

## FIVE KEY ESSENTIALS TO MAKE MAGIC HAPPEN

To sum up: Keep in mind the five necessary elements to make magic happen in cross-selling:

1. **Blended Learning:** The intertwining of onsite, seminar, and online learning systems with the right education delivered at the right times.
2. **Systematic Celebrations to Quickly Drive up Confidence and Results:** This celebration system should be designed with a "nobody left behind" plan so that the vast majority of your team members see dramatic improvement quickly.
3. **Stage-Appropriate Accountability:** This happens only after dramatic improvements in numbers. Build in a land, sea, and air approach if you want results. You *must* do this right the first time. Accountability shouldn't start until they demonstrate they can win and *are* winning.
4. **Repetition:** It's the law of learning. Our mantra is: "Until you retire, you'll be reviewing a chapter every week of the 7-Step Retail No-More-Order-Taking Sales™ process in Thank God Its Monday U™ learning platform."
5. **Ongoing Progress and Accountability:** Done correctly, accountability systems should make people feel great about themselves, not worse, which is the result that most banks get when they don't understand and manage to an organizational development system. Once you get accountability working for you, it's imperative that no excuse—core conversion, regulators coming to visit, etc.—

become an excuse for stopping the system. Revenue fixes almost all problems. Systems of revenue must never be delayed or put on the back burner.

Above all, never forget that what we do in community banking is profoundly needed in the world. Through transformational banking, we help people and their families create abundance. Transactional banking would mean we are "just another bank" and deserve no more than to match rates.

The BankShop® mystery shopping system has a special report to help you transform your mystery shopping to help you convert more "shoppers" to customers based on the 13 best practices of bank mystery shopping that drive results. You'll want to have that as you design your mystery shopping program. You can download it today at: **https://EmmerichFinancial.com/bbtoolkit**

CHAPTER SIXTEEN

# CREATING PREDICTABLE, LONG-TERM CROSS-SALES SUCCESS

*"Motivation is what gets you started. Habit is what keeps you going."*
JIM ROHN

One of the most important processes banks can build is an ongoing success system that integrates education, accountability, recognition, coaching, celebration, and practice of the retail sales process.

This responsibility goes beyond the head of retail. It is an executive team's responsibility to build and support these accountability processes. Without the executive team's involvement, accountability is seldom welcomed and embraced.

## REVENUE CORRECTS MOST PROBLEMS

When trying to improve their efficiency ratio, most banks approach the goal by cost-cutting. Often they make short-sighted decisions to cut items, such as investments in salaries, development of their people, and travel—the very "investments" that often propel a bank forward from a revenue side and help them out of a recession faster.

The *best* way to improve the efficiency ratio is through significantly increasing cross-sales. One year into the cross-sales transformation system, a plethora of banks were surprised to discover they'd moved their efficiency ratio a full 10 basis points. The remarkable part was that they weren't *even trying* to fix their efficiency ratio.

The pace of accountability matters. If people don't feel amazed with their new skills and with seeing improved results come easily, then it's too early to get serious about accountability. Accountability should happen *after* substantial successes.

Sometimes a slower approach creates dramatically faster results.

When I show executives at conferences how to apply a proprietary implementation formula to weave together all the components for holistic, predictable success, people rush to me at the breaks. They say things like: "Whoa, we've been working so hard to fix this, and I can see why we couldn't get results. We were missing the organizational psychology behind the problem."

This reaction is predictable because very few banks have executive teams that have any real mastery of the science of organizational development. It's as if they were using a hammer to secure a screw. Without the right franchise system in place that aligns the right blended education, progressive expectations, celebration, practice, and a plethora of other elements, frustration grows while results are stymied.

## HOW THE RIGHT USPS CAN IMPROVE YOUR CROSS-SALES

Effective USPs improve cross-sales dramatically. They allow you to get paid more and to increase your close rate.

However, proceed with caution. Banks that start their sales

education process before they have at least 15-20 USPs that command premium prices will create a predictable result: Their people will feel disappointed because their newfound skills "don't work."

To get a head start on creating a handful of premium USPs, consider sending a few executives to one of our events. Your executives likely know best what kind of differentiation your customers will find meaningful. Remember: The kind of USPs you need are those that cause customers to tell you: "That's worth $100,000 to me. Your fees may be higher, but hey, you're worth it!"

It brings me great joy to help a bank rise above commodity pricing. It builds great pride for team members when they also understand that their firm isn't just another "transactional" bank.

Once you have exemplary USPs, rest assured that people buy very scientifically—all you need to do is follow the right sales steps in the right order. While most sales training involves "rote questions," your people need to master reasoning skills so they can adapt their questions to the customer in front of them. They must ask the right customer needs questions based on both the type of customer in front of them and the type of product inquiry that started the conversation. Most important, they need to ask the appropriate *positioning questions* at the right stage of the sales process—the ones that make your premium price irrelevant.

The purpose of the positioning questions is to give the prospect the chance to sell *you* on why they need you—instead of you selling them. That, of course, positions you as the "financial expert" instead of a lowly vendor. Your team will enjoy the pride of knowing they're having a powerful impact on the lives of your customers and prospects.

## RIGHT PRACTICE MAKES PERFECT AS YOU REFINE THE PROCESS

After they attend our seminars, I've seen personal bankers go from never having had more than two cross-sales to having thirteen cross-sales the very next day. Of course, that isn't the norm. Most people need a tremendous amount of repetition with blending learning tools, the right systems implementation, and the right management systems to move from two to five cross-sales on average. Once they clear that bar, then they're ready to push through to seven and beyond. At that level of relationship, you can safely say: "I am my customers' trusted advisor."

When reviewing correlations to profitability, we have discovered that the highest correlation to cross-sales is having retail sales team members watch two chapters of Thank God It's Monday! U (TGIM U for short)—a multi-million-dollar proprietary platform of learning, communication, and accountability—every single week. Incidentally, no other leading indicator is as strong of a predictor of profitability growth as when our data science team analyzed activities and metrics and their relationship with each other.

The learning system provides proof, through testing, that people understand the content, so there isn't head nodding ahead of noncompliance. People can't do something they don't thoroughly understand.

Managers get reports weekly on their teams' learning goals and accomplishments, so they know that people aren't repeating the mistakes of the previous week, month, or year. Instead, they're learning how to do their jobs far more effectively.

After a bank has achieved an average cross-sales rate of 5-6 on new customers, only then are they ready for the next step: applying their refined process with their current top 100 customers. At this step, a substantial impact on profit happens.

We've already established that your top 100 customers likely account for all or nearly all the profit of your bank. Imagine what doubling each of those relationships could do.

But be warned: When people call on sophisticated, affluent customers too early without having mastered the process, these wealthy people often feel as though their time was wasted and the person returns to your bank without the entire relationship. As a result, it's harder to get a second appointment. Of more concern is that the customer is vulnerable to competitors if they call with the necessary sophistication to earn the entire relationship.

## REPETITION IS THE LAW OF LEARNING

Metals rust, gravity proves that what goes up must come down, and organized systems will naturally deteriorate due to entropy.

Learning is no different: You need John Wooden–type focus on learning and relearning the basics. John Wooden, arguably the best college basketball coach ever, was famous for his approach with every new team member: "Sit down, superstar. I am going to show you how to tie your shoes the right way."

A blended learning format helps in this effort: The repetition happens through virtual tools, team drills, and seminars, focusing on a process proven to double and triple cross-sales within a year. Additional onsite training and accountability are also helpful.

Researchers from the University of Iowa presented their 2018 findings regarding blended learning to the American Physiological Society (APS) Institute on Teaching and Learning, held in Madison, WI. They found that blended learning boosts grades, especially among students at risk of failing a course. Comparing a group of learners in a blended program to a traditional one, Professor Jennifer Rogers and her team found evidence that overwhelmingly supported blended learning. "Greater than 95 percent of students enrolled in the blended course section earned course grades [of] C- or higher, compared with 82 percent in the large lecture sections and 81 percent in the online sections," (Source: *Science Daily*)

## THE CONFIDENCE OF MASTERY

With a blended ongoing learning approach that gives people mastery and confidence, your bank can command such respect in your market that your people will never have to match rates again. What's more, they'll easily and consistently cross-sell more products and services than ever before.

Do you want to see how to roll out cross-sales mastery in a bank for the first time?

Watch the video at **https://EmmerichFinancial.com/bbtoolkit**

CHAPTER SEVENTEEN

# THE PREDICTIVE IMPACT OF EMOTIONAL INTELLIGENCE ON PROFITABLE REVENUE

*Lucy: "Do you think anyone ever really changes?"*
*Linus: "I've changed a lot in the last year."*
*Lucy: "I mean for the better."*

CHARLES M. SCHULTZ

Almost every problem in banking can be solved with revenue. While average-performing and low-performing banks spend their time trying to cut expenses—often by freezing salaries or cutting bonuses—high-performing banks think and act differently, and their successes leave clues.

If you could grow your assets per employee from $4 million to $8 million or more within a few years simply by increasing the productivity of your team members, improving their skills sets, and moving each person to their best use of time, would the effort be worth it?

## WHERE MOST BANKS GO WRONG

Most banks use "personality tests," if anything at all, for their hiring processes and for advising their team members regarding their career paths. Sadly, the reliability and predictability of "personality" to indicate performance is astonishing low. It is remarkable that few leaders in the banking industry understand that, as they spend money each year on testing instruments that add little value.

Most banks implement one of three solutions in the hope of finding a breakthrough to increased revenue that generates high profits. First, they hire more lenders. Second, they ask each lender to make more calls. Third, they hope one of those two plans work. (However, they rarely do.)

Research shows that only a few lenders—usually about 6 percent who have a business development profile—carry the rest of the team. Moreover, even that happens only if those 6 percent know how to implement the right sales process. Otherwise, those naturally gifted lenders sell only by matching rates, which is hardly impressive.

After these three steps play out, typically the fourth step is to repeat the first three, hoping things will work out differently the next time. They don't.

Most executive teams seem not to know other strategies that work. So, some version of the same three "steps" shows up annually on strategic plans for most banks nationwide. Regrettably, bank leaders always seem to hope for a different result with each attempt.

If you've been trying these strategies and wondering why you're not getting better results, you're not alone. Those strategies certainly sound as if they would be "common sense." What they are instead is commonly ineffective.

## SUCCESSES LEAVE CLUES

Let's look at banks that consistently attain NIM of over 5 and/or ROA of more than 2.0.

Team selling with team composition dictated by emotional assessment scores is a common practice of high-performing banks. Their results require consistently hitting growth goals for both loans and deposits with premium pricing on quality prospects. Anyone can close loans with desperate prospects—true mastery is earning premium pricing on the most desirable prospects in your market. After all, getting premium pricing is why sales positions exist. Technology and marketing can bring in and close all the leads. The only real function of a salesperson is to establish value, so that price matching is irrelevant.

## ARE YOUR BEST PEOPLE SERVING IN SALES?

As mentioned earlier, only six percent of your people have the emotional intelligence profile that correlates with attracting significant new business without giving up rate. Emotional intelligence is essentially the thinking underneath what are then predictable behaviors. It is like having long limbs and quick reflexes that provide the potential to be a great basketball player: The individual must still learn to play basketball, but begins with a much higher chance to succeed.

You can try the stick of threatening to put a lender on a performance plan, the carrot of incentive pay, or any other trick in your bag. However, only about six percent of your team members have the long limbs, height, and speedy reflexes that give them a chance to become your version of the NBA all-star—a commercial banker who loves bringing in large, profitable, premium-priced, full-relationship new clients.

The actuaries who analyze the data and correlations show that a low-risk sales profile will outsell a medium-risk profile by over 400 percent! It's hard to imagine how banks continue to exist without having this knowledge at their fingertips when they hire.

This doesn't mean you should fire the other 94 percent who are not business development profiles. Those with other profiles (that is, the minimum profile to be in sales) can sell very well on teams using a tightly structured and well-executed sales process designed to get premium pricing, IF they have a profile that shows they will respect a process and not deviate. If they don't have that minimum sales profile, the cost of mental anguish to them and lost sales to you can crush your profitability. Given the right role on teams, though, every individual can win due to the magic of synergy.

Of course, it isn't just revenue positions that create results for your bank. By looking at your Human Capital Audit, you will discover where you can improve your bank's performance. Is the results orientation score for your executive team low? If so, they are likely to overthink everything and get nothing done on time without convening Congress before making each decision.

Do you have errors in your operations team? It's likely that too many have a high results orientation score. That means many of them would be far better suited to a sales position within the bank, whereby they can use their gift appropriately, as opposed to having it be a burden.

Do you have people who won't ask for premium pricing because they wear their hearts on their sleeves, making bad loans to "help good people?" Their Intuition and Empathy scores are possibly too high for that position. It's likely they won't change, so they'd be better served in a job whereby they can use those high scores as an asset to serve people.

A delightful and well-loved young woman was failing miserably as the compliance officer of a bank. In fact, the bank received several fines because of her inattention to procedure. The president of the bank called to share how much they enjoyed her, but how it wasn't working out to have her in that position. When her scores were reviewed with our emotional intelligence experts, it was clear that she would be low risk as a personal banker. She was excited to take on that position. The executive team was even more excited to see that she not only became the bank's top-performing personal banker the very first month in the new position, but she also sustained level of performance for years.

The list goes on and on: Almost every problem in your bank

can be solved far more sustainably by getting every department within "low risk range" on your Human Capital Audit. This is truly one of the low-hanging-fruit opportunities that most banks aren't even aware exists, as they struggle to improve the performance of their team.

For access to a complimentary benchmark of the 104 different positions in community banking and the correlations to performance for each, go to:
**https://EmmerichFinancial.com/bbtoolkit**

In your hands, you have the blueprint to transform the performance of your bank to prosper and remain independent.

Stop overthinking…start doing.

In the words of Tina Fey, "You can't be that kid standing at the top of the waterslide, overthinking it. You have to go down the chute."

Enjoy the ride…

ABOUT THE AUTHOR

# ROXANNE EMMERICH

### Often Called the "One-Woman Economic Recovery Program"

A management consultant with 30 years of experience and a three-time Entrepreneur of the Year Award winner, Roxanne has proven that companies grow when their people grow as people. *In the first three years of working with her team, most of her clients more than double their profits!*

Roxanne shows organizations and their teams how to replace the "business as usual" of excuses, whining, blaming, gossip, and frenzied busy-work with profit- and growth-creating results and personal transformation. She helps employees experience exponential growth by teaching them how to create new skillsets, mindsets, and more enlightened ways of being. CEOs often refer to her immediate impact on their teams as "miraculous."

### In-Demand Leadership Consultant

Roxanne has consulted with half of the nation's top 1% performing financial institutions, including the executive teams of hundreds of community banks, graduate schools of banking, Fortune 500 companies, and every banking industry association.

### Hall of Fame Keynote Speaker

She has been inducted into the National Speakers Hall of Fame® and has given more than 3,000 speeches to audiences in virtually every industry. She has been recognized by *Sales and Marketing*

*Management* magazine as one of the top 12 most requested speakers in the country for her ability to transform organizations and instill a "bring it on" attitude. *Successful Meetings* magazine recognized her as the top speaker nationally on organizational change and communication.

### Founder of Thank God It's Monday U™ (TGIM-U™)

TGIM-U™ is a multimillion-dollar learning, accountability, and communication platform that has CEOs raving about the performance improvements it brings. The platform provides businesses with the templates, processes, education, and systems to advance profit and growth needles while instilling new confidence in employees. Team members learn that it is both simple and fun to understand how they tie to profit every quarter, month, week, and day.

### Best-Selling Author

Roxanne is the ***New York Times, Wall Street Journal, Businessweek, Amazon***, and international bestselling author of ***Thank God It's Monday***®, which takes organizations to levels of performance they never before dreamed possible.

### Philanthropist

She's the recipient of the Nido Qubein Philanthropist of the Year Award for her work building schools in Africa and helping children lift themselves out of poverty through education.

### From a Dairy Farmer to Successful Entrepreneur

Chosen as the distinguished alumna of the University of Wisconsin, Roxanne is also the Editor in Chief of *Extraordinary Banker*® magazine. She is the founder of the Permission to Be Extraordinary® Summit, an executive breakthrough leadership development program run by her company, The Emmerich Group, which many top executives refer to as the most career-altering days of their professional lives. Roxanne resides in Florida with her husband.

# INDEX

## K



## L



## M



## N



## P



## R



## S